Horace Field

Heroism; or, God our Father, Omnipotent, Omniscient, Omnipresent

Horace Field

Heroism; or, God our Father, Omnipotent, Omniscient, Omnipresent

ISBN/EAN: 9783337186913

Printed in Europe, USA, Canada, Australia, Japan

Cover: Foto ©Lupo / pixelio.de

More available books at **www.hansebooks.com**

HEROISM.

" LORD, shall sin work Thee shame,
To cloud Thy glorious Name?
No; Thou art so good and just,
Sin and sorrow serve Thee must:
While they last and when they die,
Thou art hope, Thou victory.

" The cross and sepulchre
On love the crown confer;
Suffering has vanquished pain,
Dying has made death a gain:
Wicked hands but wrought their deed,
That a Saviour might succeed."

    REV. THOMAS T. LYNCH, *The Rivulet*, six.

HEROISM;

OR,

GOD OUR FATHER, OMNIPOTENT, OMNISCIENT, OMNIPRESENT.

BY

HORACE FIELD, B.A. LOND.

"Blessed are ye, when men shall revile you, and persecute you, and shall say all manner of evil against you falsely, for my sake. Rejoice, and be exceeding glad: for great is your reward in heaven."—MATT. v. 11, 12.

"The desire to benefit others without a view to reward constitutes heaven in man."—NEW JERUSALEM AND ITS HEAVENLY DOCTRINE, No. 105.

DON QUIXOTE—"I tell thee, brother Panza, that there is no remembrance which time does not obliterate, nor pain which death does not terminate."

SANCHO PANZA—"But what greater misfortune can there be than that which waits for time to cure and for death to end?"

LONDON:
LONGMANS, GREEN, READER, & DYER.
1867.

GLASGOW:
PRINTED BY BELL AND BAIN,
MITCHELL STREET.

DEDICATION.

———:o:———

TO

THE BRIDEGROOM AND THE BRIDE,

THE LAMB AND THE LAMB'S WIFE,

IN WHOSE MARRIAGE

"Thou shalt be a crown of glory in the hand of Jehovah, and a royal diadem in the hand of thy God; thou shalt no more be termed Forsaken, neither shall thy land any more be termed Desolate."

CONTENTS.

	PAGE
PROLOGUE,	xi

INTRODUCTION.

The power of the Omnipotent limited by His own laws, ... 1
One mode of reconciling foreknowledge and free-will—Not satisfactory—The apparent possession of free-will no argument for believing in it, . . 2
Another mode of reconciliation—God's government so obvious that men must be gifted with a seeming freedom only, ... 3
God all in all—Man but an appearance—The devil God's agent, ... 4
Application—Each man at all times alone with God, meeting Him only, and acting only the part He appoints—All arranged as it is, that man may seem to possess powers God cannot delegate, . 5
Men mere actors, ... 6
   Mere puppets in God's sight, ... 7
   But intended to feel as free men—This view a comfort to the weary and heart-sore, . . 8

	PAGE
The existence of evil—Heaven and hell,	9
Angels and devils may both be happy when in suitable worlds—Familiarly illustrated,	10
God's goodness therefore justified,	11
Reasons for this double creation,	12
The gift of free-will,	13
Recapitulation of my theme,	14
The views stated, those commonly held—Our feeling of freedom as real as the rest of our being,	15
Free-will, therefore, practically a reality—Seeming imperfections in God's works necessary to their perfection,	16
God Himself, placed as we are, deluded like ourselves,	17

ON EVIL.

The good the evil man's presence brings to the good man,	18
Affords a field for the exercise of true nobleness,	19
Illustrated in Christ's life and death,	20
Dimness of vision sufficient alone to produce a world where self-sacrifice is possible,	21
The evil man's presence gives a priestly office to the good man,	24
The good the good man's presence brings to the evil man—The battle of life an inner one,	25
The result of contagion—This battle gives a seeming freedom to the evil man,	26
The evil man's destiny wretched only in the eyes of the good man,	27
Evil thoughts by God's inspiration consistent with what we observe about us,	28

	PAGE
Lies consistent with certain natures,	30
And may therefore be inspired direct by God if those natures subserve good ends—The good man and bad man each marked indelibly with his own nature,	32
A devil as like a creature of God's make as a tiger—Freedom from the devil to be obtained only by daring him,	33
And this may be done fearlessly, because he is but God in disguise,	34

ON GOOD.

The good man the blessing of creation,	35
Our life an imitation of Christ—Two periods in Christ's life—The first, life in the world,	36
The second, life with the good only—Christ's life as in the first period may be the life in us,	37
In the first period our Lord the teacher of both good and bad,	38
In the second, of the good only—Most men called to minister to good and bad,	39
And then can but embody the spirit of much of Christ's teaching,	40
The institutions of the world depend for their existence on the presence of bad men,	41
Men like Edward Irving wanted from time to time,	42
They are willing to be martyrs—Hell hateful only so long as we are subject to its influence,	43
The evil race not hateful, but to be resisted to the death,	44

	PAGE
No truce with the devil,	45
The in-dyed nature of the evil race,	46
Their future reformation unlikely,	48
The good effects, on the good, of their incurability,	49
No need for the evil race in heaven—They have no power to credit any motive except self-interest,	50
Must be kept at arm's-length,	52
The races, though quite distinct, indistinguishable by us—We may hence be calling down future blessings where now greeted only by curses,	53
Delusions by direct inspiration from God,	55
As credible as by His permission only,	56
The nobility they produce,	57

ON FREE-WILL.

Man, the harp; God, the harper—Love, a gift from God,	59
So also all other powers, the desire for every seemingly free act—The world within and without in the form of freedom,	60
Seeming freedom as good as real freedom—Seemingly free acts but few,	61
Not much, therefore, has to be resigned in order to find our Father everywhere—The doctrine does not lead to idleness,	62
But to prayer in action,	63
The sonship of God and repose in Him,	64
If our meditations are for good, we are of the good; if for evil, of the evil: in either case may trust in God,	65
"Vile" thoughts direct from God,	66
Given that we may know hell from heaven,	67

	PAGE
The counterpoise of heaven and hell, . . .	68
Conjugial love a parallel case—The acting of the woman—Delusion the essence of the love, .	69
Other contradictions in human nature, . . .	70
The wise man's mode of action, ...	71

ON PRAYER.

Prayer, God's address to Himself—An account according with the usual account, . . .	72
All prayer must be heartfelt—He sends the state of heart, ...	73
Foreknows the word that will be uttered—The object of prayer, its influence on us, ...	74
Letter to *Pall Mall Gazette*, ...	75
Earnest men love most to be used as givers, . .	77
An outer object seldom gained by prayer—Inner peace always, and thus our highest nature fed, ...	78
Of our dependence on God, an intellectual acknowledgment only necessary, ...	79
Outer gifts possible only for those abandoned in trust in God, ...	80
We cannot be so abandoned unless we believe God all in all—God no "deceiver,". . . .	81
Though he seems to create a world with the purpose of deception, ...	82
The same appearance of deceit in all ownership, .	83
The feeling of possession innate, ...	84
Through God's abandonment of Himself to us in love, ...	85
The world created through man, ...	86
God so loves us that He makes His appear ours, .	87

ON THE WORD OF GOD.

	PAGE
All words God's words,	88
But those called God's words which point exclusively heavenwards—They are recognized by their inner influence,	89
The Bible the soul's sun and shield—Its power felt as unassailable,	90
Describes all things with the eyes of the heavenly man—Judas Iscariot—Jewish history a drama,	91
Men described as puppets by our Lord,	92
Our Lord's temptation—Profane and Holy Writ,	93
Men mere puppets, a Bible truth,	94

ON LAW.

Law necessary to give us seeming independence,	95
Law in science and in human character,	96
The family a man,	97
The nation a man—This man its "ideal king,"	98
Appoints and controls the visible king—Cannot be God,	99
Must be of infernal or evenly balanced nature—Law makes God's doings appear ours,	100

CONCLUSION.

Examples,	102
Summary,	108
Epilogue,	111

Prologue.

ARGUMENT.

PROLOGUE in verse, as imaging victory over pain. Home-desolation the origin of the book; such desolation, making pain, which is a mere adornment of life when endured for those we love, become unendurable, and forcing the author to search for a new home, the doors of which, when found, he feels constrained to open. Pain dealt with as incurable by us, because, although wholly unphilosophical, no one can so isolate himself as to be cured by philosophy till all men are cured; such cure, therefore, in the dim distance, if, indeed, the constitution of the world does not point to pain continuing as long as the world lasts. Our love for our Lord dependent on His having endured pain. The book shows that pain is direct from God, and traces a use in pain as pain.

A Friend and the Author.

Fr. In verse your prologue?
Auth. Yes; in measured verse
I write within, "We bear real wounds—shed tears;"
But if the wounds be borne with gladsome face,
The tears of sorrow fall as drops of dew,

And image back the sun; from sober prose
Our wounds and tears are turned to smiling
    verse.
With measured tread I therefore introduce
The limping prose of deadly deeds and sin.
    Fr. Some hundred pages, rather more, I see;
'Tis a long string of words.
    Auth. You name my thought.
The heaped up foam of a great inner tumult,
For God has willed—a will I dare not question—
To veil in clouds of weary night the sun
That lit my home, in clouds that rise no more.
Thus cold and dreary, I am forced to seek
A home where cheering sun doth shine, and I—
Without a sun to shed on me its radiance—
Yet once or twice while with my pen I watched,
Mapping the footsteps of my eager thoughts,
The dream sped round about with sob and sigh,
That I again in outer form had found
The sunshine lost. A dream! a dream! no more.
A dream where dazed I see my home re-lit
By golden veilèd sun; while o'er the hills
Love—in her train each single moment's deed—
Comes gaily trooping back, and glorious pain
High o'er the cavalcade—Love's ornament—

Swoops through the distant air with glittering
   - wing.
The grazing flocks are scared; and next, I see
The fluttering thoughts I mapped start up erect,
Then quick on bounding wing drift down the gale.
It is a dream! a bold, deceptive dream!
I have no home! One hearer wanting me,
I in the ears of many tell my tale,
And the unuttered language of content
That daily grows, to troubled watcher on
An anxious search constrained, I do transform;
And now, the house of "many mansions" found,
Alike constrained, I open its barred doors,
That all who will may enter.
   Fr. Ah, thus! on pain—
You've much, I see, on pain.
   Auth. Ay, truly, sir,
An essay written thus, and published thus,
May well be styled—like many kindred essays—
"An essay on the cause and cure of pain,"—
The pain, that daily pain, which round us wraps
An icy cloak, tell-tale of frozen lands.
   Fr. I thought you told of pain that was but
   joy,—
A joy in sober clothes?

Auth. No; you mistake.
You will not find it there. I hear of such—
I with exultant gladness hear of it;
Yet for myself and you 'tis a wild theme.
　Fr. Wild theme!
　Auth. However deep and desperate our pain,
When we reflect that He, the life of love—
The only life—directs, ordains, decrees,
Besets us round about as closely now
As when He bade the world outside assume
A very different form, despair itself—
E'en lank despair—bids us pluck courage up
And whistle away care; and when we paint
The great I AM in all His drapery,
Reflect that those whose forms lie mouldering in
The grave, whose looks were love, whose every
　　deed
Was love, shed God upon us in each look,
Breathed Him in every deed; breathed Him
　　who still
Our comfort is, our daily life, our bread.*

---

* However bold this language may seem, it pales before the words of our Lord,—"I am the bread of life . . . which cometh down from heaven, that a man may eat thereof, and not die."—"He that eateth my

Do we not know the Love that gave the looks
Is ours as much to-day.—If in
Rude husk our life is coated now, instead
Of tender rind, and we the rind desire
With very hungry eagerness, we're sure
The Perfect One so clothes Himself to-day,
That we may substance love, and gorgeous show,
In right proportion,—not love too much the show.
That God loves both, the little daisy knows:
Thus also we, He calls His children, may;
And from the Perfect One assured may be
We both are getting in the perfect way.
  Fr. 'Tis glorious, sir! how then wild theme,
    I say?
  Auth. For you and me to-day—
We're not alone—must grieve with others' grief,
Bear others' woe, weep through their ignorance.
I had but yesterday rebuke to bring,
To fiercely censure those who know no rule
But their own selfish will. To-day I bade
The mother, child in arms, and busy father,
In name of public law pull down the shed

flesh, and drinketh my blood, dwelleth in me, and I in him."—"Except ye eat the flesh of the Son of man, and drink His blood, ye have no life in you."

Whose fost'ring shelter hatched a few slight
    gains
For a penurious store. To-morrow! Well!
It has its tear laid by : for if perched up
On lofty crag we look with eagle's eye,
As clearly seeing, know we're fools to weep ;
Yet when on others we must press the yoke
We know to be no yoke, we grieve that they
Will find it gall, not be the wings of angels.
Ay, grief and pain too deeply far are round
Us piled to be pressed through to-day.
    Fr. Ah, thus!
The words just now told of their disappearance.
    Auth. Of light o'er darkness, rather sun o'er
    shade;
For though the glad Philosophy you love,
Like clear-eyed Joseph, Pharaoh's wise purveyor,
Is gathering from the fields the golden fruit,
Rich with the power to rid all men of pain,
The spacious barns, the gorgeous palace walls
In quiet splendour clad, the busy men,
The creaking trains of waggons heavy laden,
With naked eye we barely can distinguish,
So long 's the road, if broad, that leads to them !
A confined road, hemmed in on either side,

By trees that push the sun away, or, niggards,
Deal it out in thrifty threads and dots;
The road a dappled avenue doth seem,
Into whose dark, o'ershadowed entrance we
May press and dimly see far, far away,
With eyes that pierce a mist like that of ages;
The houses, barns, and all the busy scene
A living landscape blazoned by the sun.
Ah, glorious sight! But when, with shaded
    eye,
You dazèd say, "Ha! ha! I'll nearer draw,
I see the folly, sin, the ignorance,
In every mental pain; convinced I'll be
Exempt. I'll run until with shout I reach
Th' entrancing sun." You'll sadly, weeping, find
You dream a prophet's dream of other lands—
Of golden lands, not of the world we fill.
    Fr. Ah, yes! of one that we may fill.
    Auth. Not so. Not so; for we are bound, are
    chained
Immoveably to men who swarm around,—
The dull-eyed multitude, more keen to seek
The fruit at hand than scan the distant scene;
A slowly pacing cavalcade, in which
Each mortal denizen that limps the road

From earth to heaven has his own place with
    thine.
And truly, sir, to me, strange though it be,
The barns, the palaces, the gorgeous scene
Seem to recede away as rapidly
As we poor mortals shuffle after them.
    Fr. Oh, say not so!
    Auth. We can but look, not order,
And what we see with eye still open tell.
Thus in the visions of this short-lived world,
That weird-like pass before my anxious gaze,
Life here and pain I cannot disunite;
Our Lord felt pain, and hence our adoration,
Our all-absorbing love. We must feel pain,
Or whine the cry, " Am I my brother's keeper?"
But feeling pain, we may exorcise it,
Gain strength, return, feel pain again, and thus
Bleed out our lives—thus pay back life for life.
The brilliant sunshine of the distant scene
We'll thank God for with lowly head, bent
    knee.
It adds a lustre to a dark foreground,
A glorious setting to a vale of tears—
The foreground ours and the distance too;
This as the foreground's setting, and no more.

Fr. Such is your theme! And thus the icy cloak
About our loins you tie immoveably.
Cold is our lot.
Auth. 'Tis cold outside. Yet, as
In arctic lands, the glitt'ring ice itself
The great protector is of heat within.
Our God and Father is the all in all,
And piercing sorrow comes by His decree;
Life of His life, dark thorny husk, it brings
The gorgeous dowry His Spirit gives.
'Tis thus I write, this my esteem for pain.
In arms of love uplifting this strong faith,
I would with reverent care some purpose show
In sorrow's bright red line both bold and strange,
Tracking the tangled path we daily tread.
Toward the goal you seek, a tott'ring step,
Perhaps you'll say, yet even so, a step.
But to the fruit itself. Taste it and try;
If bitter, cast it forth, not angrily;
If sweet, accept, and not the sweet deny.

THURLOW ROAD, HAMPSTEAD, N.W.,
February, 1867.

Introduction.

GOD even cannot make black white, or two and two into five. Omnipotence, therefore, sets bounds to its own self in its own laws. It cannot do and undo at the same time. Imagine all things but God Chaos, and He may surely make a universe, governed by any laws He pleases; but, once made, that universe can exist only by God regarding the laws that gave it birth and continue it in existence.

If one of God's gifts to men be free-will, it is, to say the least, difficult to reconcile His foreknowledge and foreordaining of events and this holy gift,—so difficult, that men, inwardly convinced of their free-will, are fain to tamper with those prerogatives of God in order to leave room for its existence. "Great events are governed by Him," they say, "but not small."

To me this is an impossible division. If walking from London to Birmingham, we certainly seem free to choose the road on which we will walk; and yet, had we selected some other road than the one chosen, we might have lost our lives. We certainly seem free to choose whether we will walk out on a holiday or sit at home and read; and yet, had we omitted the walk, we might not have met a friend who has afterwards become our good or evil genius. If, then, the apparent possession of free-will is the reason why we believe in it, we have as much cause to put faith in the above actions being free as in any other; and yet, from these seemingly free actions, the whole course of our lives has been fashioned for good or ill. Did God govern these actions, or did we?

I altogether deny, however, that the apparent possession of free-will is any argument whatever for believing we possess it; for, if contemplation of the world about us allows us to think that all thoughts leading to acts, important and unimportant, are inspired in us directly from God, then we must allow that He can, accompanying the thought, inspire also the desire to do the acts; and we mean nothing else by being free than doing the acts we desire to do. If God, then, so deals with us, we seem to be free, while we are mere puppets in His hands.

Another theory, however, which I must mention, used to be the favourite one with me for reconciling foreknowledge and free-will. I thought that it was possible God understood our character so thoroughly that He could foretell what we should do, ourselves remaining all the while free. This theory, however, needs but to be stated to refute itself. For such knowledge implies that our character can be reduced to law,—that, given the man and the position, the act can be foretold; and thus a man and his acts become the outgrowth of the nature received at his birth and the position in which he is placed. If so, his doings result from this combination, and not from free-will.

The world seems to me so clearly under the control of some regulating power leading it steadily on to foreordained results, that I must believe in this power. I cannot, therefore, believe in free-will. We certainly seem to have it, and must therefore continually act as if we had it. This must be the result of that seeming; but it is, like our whole selves, after all, but a seeming. The only reality is God—God in heaven, God on earth, God below the earth, in air, sea, land, everywhere; and creation but an appearance, borrowing all its reality from God, its Creator, and living wholly by His breath. When I say that man himself is but an appearance, I certainly rob him of nothing in saying his free-will is of the same nature as his whole being; man but an appearance most deeply fathomed when we see God working in him and through him. God, then, must work in the evil man and the good man—in devil and in angel. If He did not, I cannot but believe, with the child, that God would destroy the devil. There must be an end gained in his existence that could not be gained without it. If God, then, allows the devil to exist for good ends, the devil is in reality God's servant, and He reigns in him.

I will apply this. The table at which I sit, the ink with which I write, the lamp that lights me, the people in the room with me, the carpeted floor, the fire, the chairs,—all spring from God's presence, and are His. The evil man I meet, the meeting with whom I dread, comes by God's direction; his angry voice and threatening language is by God's appointment; he could not speak nor look but for God's will and for God's purposes. As, then, we become wise, we feel ourselves to walk alone at all times with God. In our wisest moods we retire, as our Lord did, upon the quiet mountains of the soul, and pray alone with God; there we are, though the mouth of the scorner mock us, and the lash of the angry man strike us. As we recover strength from this lonely worship, from the perception that these things are all from God, so do we return back among men, as our Lord did, and heal by the gentle word or unsparing rebuke, as He did; and all this, with ourselves actors in it, I call a seeming, having every moment fashioned and every breath drawn out of God's will, that we may seem to be that which we cannot be,—men living independently of God; that we may seem to be that which God has no power to create in its fulness—sons of God, gifted with the divine attribute of free-will—an attribute He cannot delegate, and still keep control of the world: He cannot delegate to short-sighted men, who, if they could be so gifted, would, like the fabled Phaeton, whelm the world in ruin.

"If I understand you," it may be said, "you make men mere actors; you put a literal truth on Shakespeare's words—

> 'All the world's a stage,
> And all the men and women merely players.'"

Truly; I am pleased to find words so explicit. I am glad to have so great a seer as Shakespeare to support my theory; and now I will ask, "Were, How to create a race of creatures who should enjoy the pleasures of free-will, while free-will was a gift that could be delegated to none—were this the problem God had to solve, could He solve it otherwise than by making 'all the world a stage,' by giving to this race the feeling that they did possess what they never could possess?" and if God knew that the reins of the world must be kept in His own hands, was not this the problem? For my position is,—There is no real distinction between great events and small. Small events are but the seeds of great events, and each event jostles and hustles the other in its course. If God rules at all, therefore, He rules altogether; and man, while seeming to direct, does direct nothing. Meanwhile, we have each this seeming free-will; and, therefore, I say from my point of view, this was the problem before God; and if it be a strange problem for the Omnipotent to place before Himself, still our possession of this heavenly gift—in seeming though it be—springs only from His having placed it before Himself. Let our wonder, therefore, at least clothe itself in thankfulness.

From God's point of view, then, I say man has no independent existence. He comes into the world, he lives in the world, he goes out of the world, just as God wills and pleases; he has a seeming existence of his own, independent of God, which is not real; he has a seeming will of his own, independent of God, which is equally unreal. From man's point of view, while provided through God's goodness with power to gather food and raiment for himself, he has an existence independent of God, and a will of his own on which he can act independent of God's will. God intended man to feel this: and it is therefore certain he will, and is right he should; but while so feeling, he should acknowledge that to God this is but a seeming; or, as Swedenborg says, while acknowledging he acts from God, he should act " as of himself."

I dwell on this question so much, and propose to dwell on it at still greater length, because, for the comfort and support of the weary and heart-sore, and for the encouragement of all that is independent and Godlike in the character, I desire to make the fact that men, both good and evil, events, happy and unhappy, being by God's immediate and special appointment, we really live every moment in no other presence than the presence of God Himself; that in the noisiest and most bustling, in the most painful and most dreadful moments, we are still alone with God: the breath cannot blow upon our cheeks except

His will stirs it; the axe cannot fall upon our necks except by His appointment.

"And now, if these things be," it will be asked, "How can evil exist?" If, accompanying faith in man's free-will, there be also faith in God's foreknowledge, an answer is equally difficult; for if man was created, and his Creator knew he would fall away from Him, and evil come into the world, it must have been His intention from the beginning that this should happen. Grant God's foreknowledge, then, and the theory stated creates no new difficulty.

To answer the question, however, I must premise a little.

Heaven, as I conceive, is a place in which the neighbour is loved even better than self; hell, a place in which self is loved above all. The angel's nature is Christ's nature—one in which the love of the neighbour overbears even the love of life; the devil's nature, that of the animal, if we extract from it such faint unselfish love as animals sometimes manifest. In the angel's nature all the devil's propensities are present, as servants willingly obedient to the love of the neighbour; in the devil's nature the angelic affections are present as servants to the selfish nature.

If this be a true account of heaven and hell, why may not both angels and devils be happy, if in suitable worlds, such as heaven and hell may be? Angels, we all admit, can be happy; and if devils are but wholly selfish animals, why may not they be as happy as the animals we see about us, if suitably governed? and their government being, as it must be, through fear (love existing in them only in slavery), will ever to the angel, who is governed through love, appear the tortures of hell,—perhaps the punishments of hell less so, indeed, than its delights.

Has the reader ever unexpectedly found himself in a betting ring or a "knock out" after an auction? If so, he will probably be able to realize, with the writer, what an assembly of selfish men bent wholly on furthering their own interests resembles to us, with such unselfishness as we possess; and yet the men assembled are in the full enjoyment of their own delights, and are probably none of them wholly abandoned to self. A feeling of shrinking disgust, similar to that felt in the betting ring and in the "knock out," I have also felt when some highly gambling nature has stumbled unexpectedly into a whist party; and from these experiences have been able to form a conception of what hell must seem to an angel,—what a place of utter repulsion, punishment, and torment; while to the devil himself it may be the place of his delight. Now, if devils may be happy in their home—happier, because more intelligent, than the most intelligent of the animals about us—the goodness of God is fully justified in their creation. If their creation be needful for His purposes, and if for these purposes those destined for heaven and for hell be gifted with a common form, and so mixed together that our blindness cannot do otherwise than call them all by the common name of men,—nay, if in their origin they be so much alike that it is a mere question for each whether the higher or the lower faculties shall gain pre-eminence,—why not, and yet God's goodness shine forth still undimmed? If in the end each attains a state in which his nature is fully satisfied, can any complain, because, seeming to start so equally, such different destinies await them,—an endless day the one—the other an endless night? Tears may be shed over the course of the devil as he appears to the dim eyes of the angel, and yet God be justified;—Christ utter His passionate lament over Jerusalem, "O Jerusalem, Jerusalem, thou that killest the prophets, and stonest them which are sent unto thee, how often would I have gathered thy children together, even as a hen gathereth her chickens under her wings, and ye would not! Behold, your house is left unto you desolate," and yet God's goodness be justified.*

And now, if it be asked, wherefore this double creation? — without feeling that the theory which brings into prominence the idea of God omnipotent, omniscient, omnipresent, would be invalidated if I gave no answer—I yet will give such answer as I can.

The feeling that we possess free-will—that we

* Such an address we must always remember is made to the mixed multitude, and may, in God's mighty drama, serve as the trumpet-call at which the heaven-bound spring to their destiny.

are able to do as we please—that we can act and refuse to act—that we invent, make and unmake—that we can be good or evil,—however illusory this feeling may be—however much we do but follow an instinct in all things,—I call the heavenly gift which makes us seem to ourselves capable of becoming the sons of God in a sense similar to that in which we are sons of earthly parents; and this feeling, through the mingled constitution of the world—made up of incipient angels and devils, and all the evils and trials this mixture brings—becomes so real, so ineffaceable,—we seem so distinctly to have ourselves chosen good or evil,—that while intellectually we acknowledge God is all in all, and men and their free-will mere appearance, we cannot forbear to think and act as if gifted with what God can but give in appearance; for God must be and remain all in all,— must have every smallest insect, every heavenly orb, each seemingly unimportant thought, and each life-guiding resolution, alike beneath His control.

I need now to pause and encourage myself in my seemingly ungrateful task of persuading men to step down from the lofty pedestal of an independent being. If I persuade to the truth, I might doubtless rest well assured of good consequences, did I foresee none; but with this assurance only I doubt me I should still remain silent. The feeling that we stand so lonely in our bitterest sorrows, so unapproachable, so powerless to receive comfort from our fellow-men—even as our Lord and Master was lonely—has driven me to wail, till to the shrill echo of my grief has succeeded the voice of God; and now, perforce, I must speak. I must find Him everywhere, or I can find no comfort. I must feel that He it is who bids the angry man beat me down with his insulting words; or my grief to have to face them, for ends so vain as that of carrying on existence here, becomes unbearable; but if every word and tone spring out of God's permission and appointment,—if it be, in fact, God's voice and tone,—what need we fear? for then we are assured it is for good ends it comes; then do we ever gaze into the face of God, are upheld by His embrace, which, though it may destroy this body, yet, so destroying it, gives, in the heroism called forth, a gift attainable only through the torture of the flame and at the point of the sword. Amen. Even so, my Father.

When Mrs. Oliphant writes of Major Ochterlony, shot in war—" A chance bullet, which most likely had been fired without any purpose at all, had done its appointed office in Major Ochterlony's brave, tender, honest bosom "—what does she assert more than most men and women would assert; and if there be no distinction between great things and small, what do I assert more than she? But for the overshadowing faith in free-will, which, in the vain effort to save itself, feigns them to be straws, the angry look and angry word must be alike confessed God's look and word. Surely the reconciliation of these differences is, that God gives us <u>the appearance of free-will without the reality.</u>

On the stage, however, on which we enact parts seemingly our own, but in reality parts every word and deed in which God makes us stand up, and speak, and act, wounds draw blood, pain causes suffering, there is scorn, contempt, crucifixion, death—all to us as real, though no more real than our seeming possession of free-will.

The conclusion reached, then, is, that in God's eyesight we have no free-will; in our own, we possess free-will as certainly as we suffer scorn, contempt, crucifixion, death; just as to the unerring eye the earth is seen to revolve on its own axis, while to our uncorrected vision the sun unmistakeably revolves round the earth. Henceforth, then, while claiming God to reign in all things, be the cause of all things great and small, I need no longer, for daily purposes, speak of free-will as a seeming, but as a possession.

And now it may be said, "God's works are perfect. It is therefore impossible that this world—a world so manifestly imperfect that most men's daily reading is mainly of reforms and changes needed—it is impossible such a world can be wholly His in what needs reform and in what we would leave untouched." I reply, "This world's perfection requires these things we call imperfect." Our idea of God is formed on observation of His works, within and without. The plants and trees are His.

Do we call them perfect? They have often deformed leaves and flowers, and leaves and flowers eaten in part or wholly. We, to feed ourselves, contribute to these deformities. Are not His works for use? and if use does what we call deform them, should not they be deformed? I believe God's works to be wholly perfect for the end designed—an end that, for a time at least, needs the existence of what to our short-sighted vision seems imperfection.

Here I may remark, that when such a discovery dawns on the mind as that, while seeming to possess free-will, we are really but doers of God's will, the appearance of God in the world in the person of His son, who laboured, and loved, and spoke, and wept, and suffered, and was affected by delusive appearances, like ourselves, gives to our perceptions a local habitation and a name—shows that even God Himself, placed as we are, thinks, feels, acts, weeps, and suffers like ourselves, throws a heavenly radiance of reality round our acting.

On Evil.

CLAIMING, then, that every word the bad man utters is really God's word, I feel called on to point out more plainly the good the evil man's presence brings to the good man. I have hinted at this good in my introductory remarks, and I will now dwell on it at greater length.

I am sure I speak the faith of all that is worthy when I say "that man alone is enthroned in our hearts who, having to go through contention and drive men to perform their duty, feels that, should he shrink from their anger, contempt, and threats, he is unworthy to press with his lips the lips he loves—that he dare not couple in thought his own image and the loved one's, unless he dares, without anxiety or fear, in calmness of spirit, meet this anger and contempt. Thus to feel is alone to be loveable and worthy to love."

We might be thus brave, we might be thus gifted with calm courage, like our Lord's, and have no occasion for its exercise, but we could not be assured of such gifts without the occasion; and this occasion we owe to the existence of evil. Are we not indeed, then, debtors to the evil propensities in men, which give such a field for the exercise of true nobleness—a field that could not exist but for them? And, if assured that the ultimate destiny of the evil man is one in which himself delights, may we not gladly praise God for his existence, and that we have been thought worthy to be trained in the fiery furnace his presence brings; and when our weekly trials come round, rejoice if a "sensitive nature" has not led us to find a way of escape from them; but has, instead, allowed itself to become servant to the heroic nature, and tempered with its gentleness the deeds of those that dare not press the lips they love unless their soul lies open to the beams of the heroism they adore?

The bad genius in a play is said to be always the cause of its interest, and this is as true in real life. In both, our good sympathies are enlisted by the sight of noble character, not exhibited in words or looks alone, but also in deeds—deeds that are possible only because of the existence of evil. Christ died upon the cross because there were evil men in the world to crucify Him; and had He not died, how could our adoration have gathered round Him as it now does?—how would it have been possible for the invisible Father to have poured His Holy Spirit into us—absorb our life in the life that flows from within—were it not for the love with which we are drawn to the visible Son embracing our whole nature, by exhibiting in the life He lived, crowned by the death He suffered, a love for us that has no flaw or blemish? The Lamb of God! Oh, what an image! but how comparatively inexpressive, had not the Lamb, depicting God in the world, lived and roamed fearlessly amid beasts of prey.

To the orthodox this may seem a fearful doctrine, and yet they claim the redemption of the world to have been effected by God sacrificing His Son. They therefore make the Jews God's executioners, and thus they claim the savage nature of the Jews to be one stone in the temple of our redemption: but for this nature this world-saving sacrifice could not have been effected. Of what avail Christ's appearance in the world if no executioner had been forthcoming?

If we love our neighbours as ourselves, or more than ourselves, our every deed partakes of the nature of self-sacrifice; for all we do is as all God does—so far as we can see,—full of regard and love to others; and, in a world filled with beings in whom the love of the neighbour was pre-eminent, there would still be occasion for self-sacrifice if, without being subject to evil propensities, they are yet subject to dimness of vision; for in such a world two persons not electrically alive to the state of things about them, dim in discerning God's purposes, may desire, and for a time pursue, after the same end, and we can easily see how much that is gentle, loveable, and full of self-sacrifice may be displayed in the desire of each noiselessly to withdraw out of the other's way when the perception of their mutual pursuit dawns upon them. If, in speaking of such a world as I describe, I may compare small things to great, by bringing forward the interests of this world in which we live, I shall perhaps illustrate my remarks better by filling up yon general suggestion with the particular case so often seized on by play-writers and novelists, of two men with their thoughts turned lovingly toward one woman. If to one of these men the fact that the sunlight from this daughter of God warms with a special heat the bosom of the other, and lights his footsteps, becomes suddenly revealed, how noiselessly would he step aside!—how chokingly would he keep back the expression of his own inarticulate yearning!—beneath how deep a shadow would he anxiously watch the words, the looks, the gestures, the steps of that woman and that man, until convinced that his duty and highest delight bid him step out of the shade, or withdraw for ever from a pursuit on which his dull vision only has allowed him to enter! This is a case of self-sacrifice where no evil is present; and so peaceful, so calm, so full of joy does a world in which such self-sacrifice is alone called for appear to me, that I yearn for it with a sort of broken heart. Nor am I ashamed, for in shrinking from this every-day life with its scorn and deadly deeds, I can shelter myself beneath an all-absorbing example. I speak of Him who uttered the words, "O my Father, if it be possible, let this cup pass from me." Ay, even so. I am stronger than I was. I love heroism better than I did. My spiritual muscles are more vigorous and hardened; and yet yonder is my prayer, and the response God seems to give—"Except ye eat the flesh of the Son of Man, and drink His blood, ye have no life in you."

From my visions I put my life again into God's hands and pass on.

I have pointed out the good I consider evil to effect in the world—its presence here making possible heroism and self-sacrifice even to the bearing of bodily torture and the loss of bodily life. I must now mention another good.

The presence of evil men in the world on

their road to a region which is, to the angelic vision, one of unutterable anguish, and the fact that these men are undiscernible, either by us or themselves, gives a missionary character—a kind of priestly office—to all who endeavour to labour for God alone. Although we say God is all in all, and has foreordained, predestined all things, yet the characters we have to play among each other, in His work, are given to us to seem* real and earnest—as real and earnest as our own being, with all its joys and sorrows,—a being, indeed, bound up inseparably with our acts. By this intermixture, therefore, of good and evil, we can be made to seem to ourselves to be bringing about that highest of all results, the redemption of men. Every man to whom it is given to seem to labour earnestly in all things in God's service, seems to himself in every act to spread abroad

---

* I have used the words "given to us to seem," or similar words, where I felt the key-note of the essay again needed striking. Though I consider them the correct words to use throughout, I feel myself no more bound to use them than, as I have already remarked, I am bound to use similar words when speaking of the sun's apparent orbit round the earth.

God's Spirit, to be a light expelling darkness from the world about him, and to manifest the power and peace of the kingdom of God. No enjoyment with which we can be gifted is so high as this,—not that this excludes other enjoyments, but rules over them: it occupies the first place. The hearts of those destined for heaven come to feel that, for the sake of this enjoyment, "brother, and sister, and mother," must all be deserted, if need be; nay, indeed, that if their nature be not nourished on this food, it becomes a nature in which a brother's, sister's, mother's love can never grow; that as God is our Father, so the love of the work in which we are God's most immediate agents is father to all other loves.

The seeming battle in the good man, which God produces in the world by the intermixture of good and evil, is effected by the selfish propensities in the evil man seeming to rouse the selfish propensities in the good man, and make them endeavour to obtain the mastery; and the good result this has upon the good man, in giving occasion for a seeming heroism and self-sacrifice I have already dwelt on. Now, the effect of the missionary work of the good man—the result of the contagion of his unselfishness—in like manner gives occasion to a seeming animation of the good qualities in the selfish man, which is felt by him also as a battle, with all its pain and fear. And now, it may be asked, what is the good effect on the evil man of this painful contention? for we may be well assured that God's work is so perfect that the evil man, if used for the good man's good, produces also good to himself in his very use. No one thing is made for the mere enjoyment of another,—like the pieces of a puzzle, each fits in its place exactly,—and they mutually bless each other. And does not the evil man, like the good man, receive the gift of a seeming free-will through contact with his enemy? If a seeming choice between good and evil lay not before him, a choice in which his seeming decision is made among throes and struggles of his soul, how could he suppose himself gifted with that gift which spreads a glory round the devil's head, and makes him seem to adopt his own destiny by his own selection? Peace is arrived at in both—in the evil man and in the good—when God sees well to bring contention in the soul to an end, by letting each, without further struggle, travel direct onward to the kingdom destined for him; and they carry, as the chief reward of wounds dealt and received, the conviction, indelibly marked upon them, that they have chosen freely, and are still free to choose; and if to the bright angel, rising ever to greater heights of unselfishness, to whom with increased intelligence the gift of more fully comprehending God and His ways can be continually given, the destiny of the devil appear to be to lower and lower depths of misery, the reason is, that the meat of the one is the poison of the other; the one roams over the boundless sphere in which God's unselfish presence is gloried in, and felt as, the life-giving warmth, the circling blood; the other revolves only in the narrow sphere bounded by his selfhood. To the angel, the selfishness of the devil is ever hateful, as the real enemy in his soul which he has had to overcome, and which the presence of the devil in the world served to magnetize; the devil himself is never hated or hateful, for he is obedient only to the nature in him; and while regarded as in God's hands and beneath His control, is indeed transformed into an angel, producing light by the contact of his darkness with the soul.

A difficulty here occurs. However useful the evil man may be, how can God's Spirit produce in him "evil thoughts, murders, adulteries, fornications, thefts, false witness, blasphemies?"

God has certainly made the evil man, and as certainly, it would seem, must, when He made him, have known what he would do. His evil words and deeds, then, must have been intended; and if so, there is some deeper mystery in the matter than appears on the surface. God gives life to the animals about us, the whole career of many of whom is murder and every animal act; and we feel no offence at this, because we see they are without a sense of sin. If it be life direct from God in them that does all these things, the things are not things we would do, but it is right enough for them,—

> "Let dogs delight to bark and bite,
> For God hath made them so;
> Let bears and lions growl and fight,
> For 'tis their nature too."

And when we come to evil thoughts, deceit, and lies, ought we to consider them harmful in a nature which believed everything should be subservient to it, which considered no one derived any right to anything except through itself, which held the neighbour altogether as a thing of nought, to whom no regard beyond that of necessity and convenience need be paid? We may say the nature is a very detestable nature,—as we may also say of the animal,—and that it must surely be subservient to some far higher purpose than its own existence—as is probably the case; but if God, for good ends, has seen well to create such a nature, we shall not feel there is any incongruity in His animating it with every appropriate thought, and making it bring forth every lie that need be spoken for any purposes He may have in view.

A lie! not simply by God's permission, but by His direction, as the result of the inbreathing of His Spirit! How can this be? Well! a lie. There are creatures we can imagine, I say, to whose natures a lie belongs, with whose natures it is consistent; to be the natural product of whose natures we feel no offence.

The reason a lie is a crime is two-fold. 1st. Because it is an offence against the neighbour. 2nd. Because it is an offence against God.

Every lie told for self-interest is an offence against both God and the neighbour. A lie told simply to spare the neighbour or his feelings springs out of no hatred to the neighbour, but really out of love for him—short-sighted, doubtless, but still love for him. Such a lie is, however, an offence against God, because it proceeds on the assumption that the world and its events are badly managed; that we could bring about better results than God can; that it would have been far kinder to the neighbour if the event concealed or misrepresented had not happened as it did happen, or not happened just then. Let me refer, in particular, to a lie told to spare a person dangerously ill, or to such a lie as the one often seized on in novels, where, perhaps, a sister thus saves her brother from undeserved imprisonment or death. Such lies appear offences against God only; but against Him they are distinct offences. They cast a slur upon His government, and can never be spoken by those who love and trust Him.

Now, if we imagine a creature that does not believe in a God, and who, regardless of his neighbour, except so far as he subserves his own interest, thinks it right

> "That they should take who have the power,
> And they should keep who can "—

of such a creature, a lie is a proper outbirth; and if you say, "I cannot imagine such a one;" I say, look at the animals about you. If a cat could speak, would not she tell lies to catch the sparrow? Look at the animals about you, and endow their natures with intelligence and speech,—of course, a devil is the result, but a being with whose nature a lie is no inconsistency; and granting always that they subserve good ends—turned wild among higher spiritual natures, to be driven by them from all hypocrisies, and tamed into the control of such laws as those of political economy, if they but serve good ends, why may not God's Spirit express itself through them in lies and deceit? Nay, my good, good man! do not misunderstand. They are not like you; they are of another race, a different species—Cain's children from their birth. Thy destiny is light, the glory of God; their destiny, the fate they want, the home they long for—their kingdom of rest, and peace, and quietness, where they may tell lies among their fellows, and none give them an uneasy conscience, as you would; their kingdom is to thine, the flicker of gas lamps amid fetid smells, to the glow of mid-day sunshine, and the airy fragrance of flowers.

This matter is very important, but I think the whole difficulty in understanding it will be removed if we keep clearly before us that the embryo devil and embryo angel, though here inscrutably mixed together, are each indelibly marked—one with his blackness, the other with his light; and though so alike to our eyes, are of natures tending in directions diametrically opposite.

If I met a tiger in the jungle, a crocodile on the Nile, a bear in the Polar seas, my fear of them would not make me doubt that I met a creature of God's making; and why should I doubt if I meet a devil in the streets, or if he comes into my office, and sits down on my chair, and would play all his devilish pranks on me, try to trap me into some confession on which he can get up a case to accuse me of negligence and my employer of rapacity, and so save for his pocket the few pounds justly due from him? Are his pranks any more savage or cruel than those of the tiger? They may indeed result in effects more cruel, for he has power far more subtle; but do they spring from a nature different, except in the intelligence by which it guides itself in the desire to feast upon my ruin?

Do we wish to be free from the devil? We can but be rid of him by braving him, by bearing straight onward in our course, and leaving him to do the worst; remembering that that worst may indeed bring to us contempt, scorn, crucifixion, the seeming deprivation of every outer thing, those pangs which in the world God has made precede the birth of the angel in our bosom. Take God's right hand, and fear not. He looks out on thee in every gentle smile, beneath every frowning brow. He gives the kiss, and He directs the blow that kills away from thee the mortal, the evil, the perishable. Look with a piercing eye through the devil who sits there, and behold it is God, thy friend, thou seest wrapped in that lawless nature; 'tis God, thy Father, who loves thee so that He will make a hero of thee.

On Good.

AND Good! Dear Friend! Does my page brighten to see thy glorious name head it; and having greeted evil with so many words of welcome, have I none left for thee? Thou that makest creation glorious, at whose touch the hills are clad with verdure; who nourishest the evil man, although his nature is thy opposite; who restrainest his hand, that in his blind selfishness he may not destroy the herbage from the hill-side on which he feeds; who givest him all that can be given; who givest him the greatest gift of all, defence against himself, by pouring into his shelves and dunning into his understanding the teachings of political economy, showing him that self-interest is best served when kept subservient to the interests of the community. If the evil man blesses thee by giving thee occasion for true heroism, surely thou blessest him with the convictions which make his living in society, his own existence, possible.

Our life, we read, should be an imitation of Christ.

Our life should truly be Christ's life in us, for in His life is summed up the life of every good man. His life, however, has two periods.

Of the first of these periods we know little more than that "the grace of God was upon Him," that He felt He was engaged upon His Father's business, and this general epitome, "And He went down with them [Joseph and Mary], and came to Nazareth, and was subject unto them;" "And Jesus increased in wisdom and stature, and in favour with God and man."*

---

* In my remarks on the Word of God I have pointed out that the Bible is holy, because it does not touch on the interests of the mingled race, nor of the infernal man, but addresses itself solely to the heavenly man; and therefore it is that this first period of Christ's life, in which His interests, we must suppose, were those of the mingled race, admits only of the few passing words that record it.

Of the second period we find a record in the New Testament, full enough to make that book the seed of all goodness in humanity. In this second period we find food produced by miracles. Of it we read—"Foxes have holes, and the birds of the air have nests, but the Son of man hath not where to lay His head." In it His disciples are bid—"Provide neither gold, nor silver, nor brass in your purses, nor scrip for your journey, neither two coats, neither shoes, nor yet staves: for the workman is worthy of his meat." In it, so far from growing in favour with God and man, we find the favour of God growing on our Lord, indeed, from within, yet seeming to depart from Him from without. And for man's favour, at one trying moment in His career, we find Him deserted by this altogether.

If we ask, "Of which of these periods is the life of Christ the life in us?" the answer must be for most of us, "If of either, of the first."

Christ, as He was in this first period, may be the life in us; His life, as it was in the second period, is not, probably cannot yet be: for if we ask ourselves at any moment, "How would our Lord act here?" we must think of Him as He was at the time when subject to Joseph and Mary, growing in stature and favour with God and man.

We have, of course, to judge of what He was at this period chiefly by our after knowledge of Him. We have to judge of the germ by the fruit; but back to this period our ideas must recur. We must clothe the spirit we find in the fuller record, with the form of life lived out in the shorter. Men, as we call ourselves, we must, like Job and his comforters, be content to learn of one perhaps far younger in years than ourselves. The difference between the first and second period of our Lord's life, indeed, is, in my apprehension, essentially this:— In the first period our Lord was a teacher of both the good and bad type of men. The good received a further inspiration toward goodness from Him; the bad were led by Him to recognize, in a form of life outwardly heavenly, the form best suited for the enjoyment of selfish passions.

In the first period our Lord lived among outer rewards and punishments—among offices, situations, salaries, fines, and imprisonments—as one who had to use them, and teach the right use of them—just, indeed, as we live among them; and these are institutions which dog the footsteps of the evil man, are of use only in enforcing, by means of self-interest, a life outwardly regardful of the neighbour: any teaching as to their use, therefore, can be of eternal benefit only to the occupants of the infernal kingdom.

In the second period of His life our Lord addressed Himself to the elevation of the good man, and the opening of the gate of Heaven for him. He broke away from the evil type of men altogether, painted their life in the aspect only in which it appears to the good man, acting thus on the evil man from the side of repression, not of persuasion; and hence His crucifixion and death.

I consider this account of Christ's life complete; and from it I infer that there is a humble use to which the bulk of good men are called —that of ministering to men, good and bad— by inspiring the good with something of their courage and love of God, and expounding to the evil that their deity, self-interest, is best served by doing the things the good man is led to do, and sees to be right, from the higher ground of duty; and thus lending, as it were, their eyes to the evil man, enabling him to see that which, unaided, he could never see, and that which, in a future world, will uphold a social life among intelligent and selfish beings impossible on any other foundation.

Those who fill this humble office live outwardly as they must suppose Christ lived in His earlier life, not as He bids us live in the Gospels, whenever the action inculcated is suitable only for the teaching of the heavenly man.

He, therefore, who feels that his office here is for the double purpose of teaching the hell-bound and the heaven-bound, can only embody in his actions the *spirit* of such instructions as, "Whosoever shall smite thee on thy right cheek, turn to him the other also;" "If any man will sue thee at the law, and take away thy coat, let him have thy cloak also;" "Give to him that asketh thee." The spirit of this teaching, we are sure, dwelt in Christ's actions in the days of His subjection to worldly authority, when He grew in favour with God and man; but we are also sure that such actions, if literally performed, contain the worst of lessons for the infernal man—can only encourage him in all his vices.

Just so far as we live in houses secured to us by title-deeds, take and grant leases and agreements, run up bills at the butcher's, baker's, and linen-draper's, keep balances at the banker's, institute and defend law-suits, form committees and gather subscriptions by appeals and lectures, send missionaries abroad supported by funds at home, and write and read books on "How to make the best of both worlds,"—just so far we become teachers by word and deed of lessons understood and accepted by both good and evil—of lessons the value of which to the former perishes with their life here; for we climb not to heaven on lands and houses, or on the means which procure and keep them, but by a heart free of guile;—while to the latter these lessons form the never-dying key-note of their life, for hell is maintained through the perception that a selfish world is made the best of by a life outwardly regardful of the neighbour.

A man like Edward Irving may, in his wild enthusiasm, step out of the beaten track, and startle the ears of men by denunciation of all reliance on subscriptions and committees in work he deemed especially divine, and bid men, in following the literal teaching of our Lord and the apostles, break away from all catering to the apprehension of their fellows of the evil race—a race whom God has made—and who, while they do not offend against the laws of society, have a full title to live unmolested by the heavenly man, although their every action springs from that old offender—the source of all we call evil—self-love.

I am thus friendly in speaking of evil men, for God created them; but so also did He that " Enthusiasm of Humanity " which already once has filled the world with heavenly light, and ever, from time to time, may be needed to shine out afresh, and separate good from evil.

Any of us may be called, as our Lord was, to appeal to the good alone by persuasion, to the evil by denunciation and repression;

and if so called, of this we may be assured, we shall not scruple to quit houses held by title-deeds, to have done with bankers' balances, the defence of the law, subscriptions and appeals, and to abandon ourselves wholly to God, as did our Lord, as our Lord bade His disciples do.

If we thus feel called, may God speed us in our holy work, make us content to have our life wrapped in a maze incomprehensible by the evil, wholly offensive to them, and willing to put on our heads the martyr's crown handed to us by God's executioners, the men of evil.

To the good man, who sees in acts their motives only, the doings of hell, so long as he regards devils as fallen men, consist of robbery, deceit, evil speaking, adultery, murder, and every crime; for however much, outwardly, the influence of heaven in such teaching as that of political economy—a science demonstrating that state of mind which is the heart of all crime, to be most fully gratified by an external subserviency to the neighbour's interest—however much outwardly such teaching may keep hell in order, the inner air and life of it must ever be crime in its essence to the good man, while he regards devils as men, or while they can influence his nature sympathetically, but no longer. I refer again to animal life. We have a cat, for which we feel much affection, till one day we see it seize on a mouse, play with it in its timorous endeavour to escape, and finally devour it. If, forgetful of the cat's nature, an unwise affection has given it any human attributes which call forth our sympathy, we are shocked by the cruel sight, and expel the cat into the darkest regions of the house. We say it is the nature of the tiger to destroy other animals, regardless of their sufferings, and even, if pressed by hunger, to eat its own offspring; and with a certain shrinking from anything so savage, we pass it by. We abhor, spurn, hate, only when we believe there is in the savage creature a higher nature he disregards in obeying his savageness. If, then, I regard a man I meet as possibly an evil man, with a nature like the tiger's, I cannot hate that man. I may resist to the death any of his doings, which, if not resisted, would call for deceit, an abandonment of trust, any unworthiness on my part ; but I cannot hate the man— I only feel that he would bring his wares to the wrong market; he would have the heaven-bound act as if they were hell-bound. His very rage at me shows that he cannot grasp my motives. The good man in the world must ever be toward the evil man like the Archangel Michael in Raphael's picture, who, with calm, stern, unruffled brow, and with a foot sparkling from the starry floor of heaven, is alighting on the prostrate form of Satan, his spear, held in both hands, he is about to thrust through the fallen form with the resistless strength of his uplifted arms, wrapped up in the momentum of his descent. There must be no truce, no terms with the devil; not because he is a devil, but because he would tear down its ramparts, and climb to heaven. Let the brow be calm, for, poor fellow! he knows no better; it is an offence, a crime, a mockery, a hypocritical pretence to withstand him: he will frighten you out of it, coax you out of it, bribe you out of it; and if he cannot, he will spurn you, and scorn you, and carry his hatred towards you to every deed he—regardful of the policeman and his own self-interest—dare.

A friend of mine, the physician to one of the London prisons—somewhat of a faithless sceptic, I confess, and so far observant of the sceptical side of things—remarked to me many years ago, with a smile of contempt, the falseness of the priestly faith, that the prisoners had qualms of conscience for their deeds. They would pretend they had, if such pretence was likely to bring them any indulgences; and their prison experience might for the future make them more cautious thieves, put a few political economical principles into their heads, make them think honesty might possibly prove the best policy; but as for being remorseful that they had robbed the poor man of his store, that they had made existence a burden to the man they had kicked and beaten, that they had made the dark hours of the night a time of almost unbearable alarm to the woman keeping house alone,—not a tithe of them but would do all they had done again to-morrow, if to-morrow it should be as possible and seem as desirable as it did yesterday. Such men are tigers, or on the high road to so become: and even Mr. Ruskin will join in blessing political economy, if their experience of this life should enable its doctrines to keep a crew like that in order.

Such are the assertions of my friend the physician; but we are, unfortunately, not reduced to dependence on his experience. Thieves and robbers do not exist among pickpockets and burglars only. We all meet them almost daily,—men who act parts to trade upon our charity; men who try to pass off their goods upon us by false pretences; men who will take advantage of any ignorance we may display as to the prices and value of things; and if we do not often meet personally "men who seek to compass the ruin of an innocent and solvent company or firm by persistent attacks on its credit, and do this for the sake of getting a higher profit on a speculative sale," * or with tradesmen who weigh with false weights or scales, and sell short measure, we read of them in the papers, and at

* Daily paper.

times hear of them at the police court, and even of their continuing the same career of robbery after conviction. We none of us doubt that habit has made these things appear hardly a crime to many, and are perfectly sure that to others exposure produces no remorse: we should, indeed, as soon expect to see St. Paul's Cathedral walk into our houses as to find the great bulk of such men refund their ill-gotten gains. I may surely, therefore, appeal to our own experience among these fair weather thieves, in confirmation of my friend the physician, and of the faith that, unless repentance be on the deathbed, these men carry their sins with them into the grave. When they reach the distant shore, does reformation wait them there? This may be. My faith as to the other life says no; and if I have shown, and shall show, that God's goodness is fully justified even if they are not reformed, and if —without appealing to any fanciful views I may hold as to the laws of the spiritual world which renders reform there impossible—I further show that their not being capable of reform re-acts to the advantage of heroism and goodness in this world, I give strong reasons for thinking their state of selfish love on leaving here is a final state.

The good effect of the evil on the good in this world springs out of collision with the good. If we believe among those we meet some have a nature to be tamed only by fear, never by forbearance, ready to the last to turn on, bite, and destroy him that forbears, far greater intensity is given to this collision than if we believe all men alike will one day thank us for every gentle deed. How much more sacred to God and His goodness is our resistance made in the one case than in the other! The former faith keeps the edge of heroism sharp and keen; the latter leaves it blunted, as in a time of peace. The former faith tends to rear the hero; and I do not think I am far wrong in stating that the latter points, as its highest result, to an expressionless character, possessed of a gentleness which we feel unreal, because satisfied that it would never bear contact with actual life—a character often the seeming beau-ideal of the clergyman. I need not ask which of these characters a good man in actual life must bear, nor to which of them the creation of God—who makes man in His own image—is most likely to point.

It is, again, absurd to say, "God would not make a creature so like a man remain a devil for ever: He would not so thin the family of heaven." If such a creature be necessary in the creation—the spiritual birth of the angel—why not? and as to reducing the family of heaven, this is a thing of which we cannot talk. Heaven must be peopled at that rate, and that rate only, which God sees needful. He could surely make good men grow on trees, or multiply like rabbits, were it fitting, without using the race of evil men for the purpose of filling heaven. Let them go to the dark homes in which they delight. They have a use, be assured, no good man can fulfil.

I assert, then, that the world, peopled so seemingly with men of one race, is, in God's eye, peopled with races diametrically opposed. If this assertion be true, those about us of the dark race not only do not, but have no power to believe in any but selfish motives. Do we find such people in the world? I believe they abound. If I am wrong, my theory falls to the ground: I admit, we are all heaven-bound.

Let the reader consider this point—a point on which, in actual life, a correct conclusion is of great moment—and, so far as his faith is concerned, abide by the result.

For myself, I find the attempt to make most of those I meet believe I am actuated by motives of duty certain to produce faith only in my hypocrisy; so certain, that I never name the word duty, even when forced officially to control men from this motive alone, but point out, that to neglect such control would be impossible for me from the worldly side only; and thus, and thus alone, can I procure a hearing.

I could name a number of men, the greater part of whom, I am sure, should they stumble across this book, have no power to believe it published from any other motive than self-interest—deeply buried, perhaps, but still self-interest. They have no power to credit that, while rather shunning than caring for publicity, I yet feel impelled—dare not refuse—to court such censure and such praise as this public exposure of my faith may call forth. They might seem to credit my statement; but test their faith by any action which it would influence, and with what self-satisfied assurance would they proceed on the certainty of my motives being those of self-interest! Whatever they may seem to think, they hold in their hearts no other faith than this.

Kept at arm's length, and amid the interests they understand not catered to out of kindness of heart—which they will misread for fear or a desire for bribes—but ever held rigidly beneath the rule of a considerate justice, checked resolutely by the dread of evil consequences, they may prove manageable men, with even a jovial air about them; for manageableness and joviality then best consort with the self-interest they worship—that self-interest in respect to which we read in the parable, "The children of this world are in their generation wiser than the children of light."

If I describe a well-known race correctly, and if I say truly that heaven is a place where the love of others rules over the love of self, I describe a race that cannot be raised to heaven, for they have no eyes to see it, no hearts to understand it; their home and that of the heavenly man must be as the two poles asunder.

Dark, however, as these men with whom we meet, talk, dance, bargain, may be both here and hereafter, in the sight of God, indelibly marked, and never for a moment to be confounded with the good, they are, to our mortal vision, so mixed with the good, and undistinguishable from them, that we can draw no line of separation,—and in such close resemblance in our eyes this new advantage appears. The man so seemingly hell-bound may, after all, be heaven-bound,—we cannot tell; and we, in resistance to his pretensions, may be made the seeming means of animating in him the divine life—of giving to his heavenly nature the predominance. God may thus work out the game of life; and if we deny any merit in ourselves, the actors used—if we say that our real inner self is but passive in the whole action,—we at all events have to acknowledge that our inner self is not without its suffering—that heroism has to be born in it with pangs and throes—that the now clearly heaven-born man has reached his new state at the cost of our endurance;* and hence the keeping of the command, "Judge not, that ye be not judged;" the believing that each man we meet may be an angel in disguise comes to us enfolding the accustomed blessing —like the marshal's baton, said to be wrapped in the French soldier's knapsack. We can never tell that our very resistance is not turning the vilest enemy into the dearest friend. The separation of the hell-bound and heaven-bound "judgment" belongs to God only. As an outer fact impressing this inseparability by us with vivid force on the mind, we read that one crucified beside the Lord was a thief, who was yet pointed out as on his way to paradise.

Every thought, word, and deed is, I say, God's thought, word, and deed; and yet, as we are well aware, our thoughts—the conclusions

---

* "The Mystery of Pain" takes for its theme this result of our sufferings, and points out with much ability that, just as the sick man owes it to his sickness to feel that exertion pain which the healthy man finds pleasure, so the unregenerate man owes it to his fallen nature to find those things suffering which, if regenerate, he would feel as the pleasurable pain of exertion.

we draw from what passes through our minds—are often inaccurate.

A combination of events led me on one occasion to vary my hitherto almost constant habits. This variation, remarked on by another, induces a strange smile. I am puzzled—almost offended. A few nights after, in dreams upon my bed, I suddenly, as I think, understand the smile, and with the understanding comes a new life to all my hopes, and a perception of the value for my present purposes of the change of habit I had intended to last for one day only, and with a whirr among my thoughts, like the rising of a covey of partridges, or the rushing noise of a stream bursting into a new channel, I adopt the change of habit. All seems as I expect. I push my action on with vigour. A delusion! I misunderstood the smile, and the tender web of all my dearest hopes is torn into rags by my action. My hope rose in the air like a rocket—like a rocket it bursts; the flickering sparks descend, and all is darkness.

Similar experiences are doubtless common to all men.

The devil, some will say, deludes men thus—

not God. Ay! but if the devil be God's agent, how then?

On my theory, of course, the smile, the conclusion drawn, the daily false meditation and baseless vision, the action founded thereon, the extinction of my hopes thereby, were all intended, inevitable, the result of the direct working of God's Spirit on mine. As such delusions would result were we free, I hold it to be a necessary part of the inspiration in our minds that we should be subject to them; and to say that it is unworthy of our idea of God that He should so act directly upon us, who would so act by His intention had He given us free-will, is like saying a man who would light a train of gunpowder and then run away, that he might not see the effects of the explosion, may be more worthy than he who lights it and stands by. Besides the seeming manliness that is produced in our characters, the seeming independence is so obvious! How noble, human, loveable that character which says, "Delusions abound in my mind: I know it quite well; but I will act fearlessly all the same, on the best conclusions I can deduce; and when I do get knocked down against hard facts, I will get up again; and the staff, as I know by experience, on which I shall then rise, with an increase of trust, is faith in God, and this certainty.—Expecting easy victory, I have found hopeless defeat; if yet, though defeated, I have borne my defeat regardless of my own loss, and careful only to shield others from pain, then I have been led by the delusion to give increased faith in all I think manly, in a place where, but for the delusion, I had never appeared, and where, possibly, such influence only as has sprung from my defeat is of value." One who thus speaks is being schooled by delusions to love actions for the nobility in them, while one guided by an infallible instinct must come to love them for their outer results only.

A truce with defence! I repeat: we do not blame God for what we see in the world when we suppose men free; and if God had foreseen what would follow from freedom, and yet had ordained it, He would have been surely quite as worthy of blame as if, men not being free, He yet gives the appearance of freedom by directly inspiring all that would have followed from freedom—if He leads us to go right and to err in that way precisely in which we should have gone right and erred, had we been free.

On Free-Will.

THE man himself, then, I consider a mere sentient existence on which God operates—the harp on which He plays. We certainly experience pain and joy; we feel love and all the other emotions of the mind; and though we know by experience that some of these emotions will, as a rule, follow certain external positions in which we seem to have the power of placing ourselves, and though we seem to have a certain control over these emotions, this control takes the form alone of government and restraint. No more than we can turn one hair black or white can we cause any of these emotions to come, however much we may desire the result of their coming. Who would not reanimate in his soul the sweet influence of love, if he has once felt that influence? and yet, what longing of his can so reanimate it? We can but wait and hope. "The wind bloweth where it listeth, and thou hearest the sound thereof, but canst not tell whence it cometh and whither it goeth. So is every one that is born of the Spirit;" and every one in whose heart love is animated.

Just as we must acknowledge love and many emotions to be but gifts from God, so, I consider, we must acknowledge all other powers, thoughts, words, deeds, and acts to be direct operations of His Spirit in us, the thought leading to every seemingly free act being inspired in us, and, accompanying the thought, the desire to do the act also given, and thus all these things coming to us with a seeming freedom about them; and this world, with its varied play and emotion, its trivial and important acts, its doubts, considerations, weighings, *pro* and *con*, thus ordered that it may take the shape which free-will, if really ours, would give it—a shape, however, for ever tending more and more to the fixed peaceful form, with the calm onward movement of all our desires and deeds, which it will assume when the result of our present doubts and hesitations is reached, in the impression left ever vividly on our minds, that we are really free—an impression which, while it remains, makes us as good as free.

What is it to us, in our daily conversation and daily interests, that philosophers demonstrate the earth to revolve on its own axis, while our eyes so unmistakeably tell us that the sun goes round the earth. It is of no moment. The motion of the sun round the earth is indeed the most real motion of the two to us, until for any rare practical purpose we need correct appearances by demonstration.

How few acts of our lives do we even seem to do for ourselves! We eat food seemingly of our own free-will: once received in the stomach, all further operations upon it are deprived even of this seeming; and how multitudinous are such operations compared to the simple act of eating! We move our hands seemingly of our own free-will, and guide them to certain acts to which we seem to have carefully trained them; but beyond such acts we can do nothing with them; and the number of things they seem able to do are, to those we know they cannot do, as one grain to the sea-sand. We seem able of ourselves, with their help, to put seeds in the ground, and then no more—to gather the fruit, prepare for use or replanting, and then no more. Everywhere we seem able to do a few things ourselves, and then the whole process has confessedly to merge into God's hands.

If I say, then, that to these few seemingly free acts this freedom is but in seeming, I do not deprive much of our being of the greatly desired prerogative, and the seeming being as real as it is—indestructibly real—we may learn to be grateful that it is but a seeming, if by so acknowledging we can find our Father everywhere, in every prick of a pin, in every stroke that beheads; if we can feel that the whole web of the world is as seamless in its weaving as our Saviour's coat, as newly formed every day from God's hand as the wing of the insect that lives but for the day.

To say that this doctrine leads to idleness, is to say that God is imperfect in His doings.

It does so tend, perhaps, until we see it in its fulness—until we perceive that God acts in the world through men, and that to give any of us the desire to act, is to give also the feeling that the act is done out of our own free-will, and that till we have this feeling He does not ever work through us; or, in common parlance, God does nothing until we exert ourselves. If we desire to receive my doctrine out of love to God, that love will swell in our bosom till it becomes the soul of an activity in which our ambition is to resemble Him who, sleepless and unwearied, preserves a world in life by momentary acts of new creation—who gives life to our own souls by hourly renewing the occasion for exertion, and the heart with which to fill out the occasion. Idleness? If my doctrine presents to the soul a wider field for the love of God to occupy—a greater scope for trust in Him —idleness is blown away as by a rising wind, and the calm, peaceful desire and power for exertion fills every crevice of the soul; and in place of idleness comes that hopeful, vigorous waiting upon God which is prayer in action, and a state of mind in which the seeming independence of ourselves and our acts is received as the greatest, holiest, and most perfect of gifts. And does not this doctrine lead us to regard God as Father—pre-eminently as Father?—Father of every thought, wish, desire, hope, and deed—ay, of every fear, care, trouble,—fears, cares, and troubles created to be exorcised by a trust in Him which acknowledges Him to be all in all; for the things feared can be brought against us only to induce in us heroism and every good and noble gift, if, indeed, they are the result of His presence, if they come from Him so utterly, so direct.

There is an event—my dream by day, my hope by night—whether it will occur, God only knows; but if I believe my day dreams and my night dreams to be the effect of the sighing of His Spirit upon my soul; if I believe the schemes and plans to bring about my hopes are all of His handwriting, and that the schemes of to-morrow will be His alike, how snugly do I roll myself in my coat woven of faith in Him, and there abide the issue, assured that the result, whether like or unlike my desires, will have a glory the web and woof of which is woven out of the trust and faith I feel, which is His gift also, though the shape in which it comes to me marks it so sweetly as a thing of my own inducing.

We thus are the harps, and God the harper. In all our seeming meditations, for good or ill, it is not we who meditate, but God in us. If the meditation be for good, we are possessed of that higher nature which loves others better than ourselves; and being thus Godlike, we may be brought at last to do as God requires us to do, out of love for the deed itself. If the meditation be for evil, we are possessed of that lower animal nature which cares for self above all, and cannot therefore be kept in God's ways—ways ever regardful of the good of others—except through the fear that want of such regard will damage ourselves. We are, then, made like the leopard—the leopard so glorious in form and wonderful with his spots,—we are like animals upon whose make and maintenance God expends unfathomable skill, and being like them, we may be sure that skill as great is expended upon our make, and will be on our security and maintenance.

And yet one step further. Some dreadful thought persistently seizes upon the mind, and will not be driven away;—some horrible, debasing thought, that makes us shrink within ourselves—almost abhor ourselves—and feel it were a mercy were we dead. And do I mean that this thought is from God direct?—Even so.—Not sent for the nature of the thought itself, but for the results. Covetousness, murder, incest, are not horrible in the mere animal; God has so made them, and God has in like manner, as I understand things, so made the evil man. Let the evil man once fall wholly into his selfish or animal nature, and he will restrain himself from these things only so far as he feels his own self-interest requires him. That which in the good man is a desire for wealth, that he may bless others with it—a disregard of life as compared to higher ends—a holy love, becomes in the evil man covetousness, an indifference to murder, incest. The life of the evil man is in things every one of which is abhorrent to the good man. Form a mixed world, then, such as ours is, and give to the atmosphere which breathes from the evil a seeming power to infect the mind of the good, and of the good to infect the mind of the evil, and you immediately have a world of conflict such as ours; and if God has seen good to place us in this world, we may be sure He is not ashamed, does not shrink from His own work. We honour Him, therefore, but little, if we think He cannot, in keeping with the world in which He has placed us, blow across our souls the thoughts of the evil man, the mere animal (thoughts, remember, innocent in them), that we may see the difference between the state of the good and the evil—between heaven and hell—and rejoice with holy joy to have the hateful thought withdrawn, and heaven—if it be with its cloudy verge alone—closing once more around us. It is that we may, by intellect and experience, perceive the difference between a good and evil nature, and be able to have the love of the good inspired in our souls, that we find evil here; that we may with a seeming freedom of choice select of ourselves the thoughts which make us sons of God, angels of heaven. Swedenborg says that the existence of hell, as a counterpoise to heaven, is necessary to secure our freedom. To me this counterpoise appears to give a *seeming* freedom only. Having the two states of mind shown to us within, in the experience of our own souls—in which we perceive capacity for any evil, as well as aspiration after a goodness continually beyond our grasp—and having the fact that both capacities may be woven into living and acting characters exhibited outside us, a reality is given to the existence of both good and its opposite which is unmistakeable. Between the two we stand: we seem to be able to turn to either; to be able to have the predominating love of the one or the other inspired into our souls; we follow the inspiration of that love, become endued with the angel's nature, or with equal relief escape from the conflict and fall into the service of self when getting away from the sense of sin, we cry out with Satan, in *Paradise Lost*, "Evil, be thou my good." —

 . My statement is, then, that God Himself

directs all our movements, and so directing, gives us the feeling that we direct ourselves. There is a process so strangely parallel among our social relationships that I cannot pass it by. I refer to conjugial love. An observer of the working of the heart well knows that conjugial love springs from the woman and returns to her. It originates with the woman. It is a gift from her to the man, which he feels in himself as though he originated it, and feels this so strongly that it will even vanish away—as the woman is herself well aware—if she by acting failed to keep up this strange delusion in his mind. Shakespeare makes Rosalind relate the art employed to effect this purpose, among the other female secrets he allows her to betray under her male disguise—

"*Orl.* Fair youth, I would I could make thee believe I love.
"*Ros.* Me believe it! You may as soon make her that you love believe it; which I warrant she is apter to do than to confess she does; that is one of the points in the which women still give the lie to their consciences."

Now, the remarkable part in all this is, that the delusion in the man's mind, that he himself originates the love, is essential to the existence of the love itself; just as when doing any act at the direct bidding of God, the delusion that we do it ourselves is the heart of all social existence.

Human nature is full of such contradictions. We may say, for example, to a mischievous child, "Your whole life is needfully a cause of trouble to all about you; you ought to try, therefore, and give as little needless trouble as you can,—not that we do not all delight to take trouble for you—we should, indeed, be lost without it—but our delight will pass away if we do not see you endeavour to relieve us of all the trouble you can;" and thus desire to rob us of trouble is the only way to keep up our delight in it; and these contradictions must be in the heavenly nature, if we regard its essential life to be self-sacrifice, until they culminate in conjugial love, the essence of which is the complete absorption of the gift by the receiver, and its consequent return to the giver.

In conjugial love, then, the woman plays toward the man the part of Deity. She gives that all-engrossing heavenly love to him, accompanied by the persuasion that he himself originates it. She first selects him from among other men, and he perceives it; each advance is hers, and he feels it as his own, because he loves it; she induces the final declaration, but the man speaks the word, and heaven and earth cannot persuade him that he is not the author of it, because he pours out his whole being in it; and these persuasions she will induce in him at any cost, and will not disturb him in them —no, not at the price of life itself. And what does the wise man do when convinced of these truths? He accepts these doings on the part of the woman as of her true nature; he revels in the delusion itself thus valued by her, and thus supported as the richest jewel in her diadem, and as men thus deal with women as to conjugial love, so should the whole race deal with our Father in heaven as to free-will, —receive the inspiration to the deed, accompanied by the love for it, as His gift, and adore Him for ever that the gift thus given persuades them that they, and not God, are the authors of their acts.

ON PRAYER.

A PRAYER, then, consists of words spoken by God and addressed to Himself, listened to by us in passing, the sense seized on, its applicability to our seeming state perceived, and the words given to us with the feeling that they contain our own address to our Father, who has fashioned them as He has fashioned all things.

Is this seemingly strange account of prayer different from the account in general acceptation?

A prayer like that of the king in *Hamlet*, which, rising from his knees, he thus despairingly describes—

> "My words fly up, my thoughts remain below;
> Words without thoughts never to heaven go"—

we all, from Shakespeare onward, admit to be vain and valueless.

The prayer desired, the prayer whose efficacy is alone acknowledged, is that in which the lips express in words a prayerful state of heart. And how is such prayerful state to be procured? Not manifestly by prayer, because it must precede prayer. It is true the spirit of prayer increases in volume with the utterance of the words; but even in its increase it is felt as a gift, which can be given only to a reverential or prayerful state of heart. "The wind bloweth where it listeth, and thou hearest the sound thereof, but canst not tell whence it cometh and whither it goeth. So is every one that is born of the Spirit."

As to prayer and all spiritual states we obviously wait at all times on the Lord. He sends these states upon us as He sends His winds, as He creates us with our bodies and their several members. We may philosophize on how these states come, but we do not think of controlling them, even seemingly, except the desire for certain states be first in us. If this be so, if this desire be sent by God, and arise in us only so far as He sends it, and if He foreknows the words it will produce; if He "knoweth what things we have need of before we ask Him," then, sending the desire and knowing the result of the desire, He practically addresses Himself through us as completely on the theory of our being, generally held, as on the theory I have stated. This result must follow if we admit the initiatory prayerful desire on which all our prayerful habits and experiences are built, to originate with God, as the first Former of our being, and not with ourselves; to be born in us and breathed on us as the members of our body are born with it, and as the life-giving breath of heaven is breathed upon it.

All genuine prayer, then—all prayer that is not lip service—comes from an inward desire to address God, and such desire is God's gift to us;—may seemingly be cultivated and improved, but cannot even seemingly be initiated; and God, foreknowing all the results of such desire, addresses Himself through us in every prayer. Now, clearly, the object of such address is the influence it will have upon us, and not upon Him. In the Revelation we have the nature of prayer beautifully illustrated. The elder beside John first asks John a question, and then answers it himself. "And one of the elders answered, saying unto me, What are these which are arrayed in white robes? and whence came they? And I said unto him, Sir, thou knowest. And he said unto me, These are they which came out of great tribulation, and have washed their robes, and made them white in the blood of the Lamb." Just so God puts a question into our minds, and then Himself answers it. It is intended, in order that we may feel ourselves children of God, that inquiries and desires should arise in our mind, which take the form of prayer.

Stirred out of my usual patience by some remarks of the *Pall Mall Gazette* on the subject of prayer—a paper always wise, generally liberal, though sometimes, from my point of view, dull sighted—I recently sent them the following letter, which they did not think well to insert :—

" The *Pall Mall Gazette* seems not to recognize that prayer may be as much one of the intended results of God's laws as smoke from straw when set on fire. If God be our Father in heaven, the influence of His laws upon us must be one of their intended effects, and prayer, therefore, also, if prayer be the natural result of that influence on the child. My little child in her bed by my side wakes me several times by an unusual restlessness, seeming to betoken some coming illness; at first irritable, a holier influence comes over me. I wake more fully, and I say, 'O God, my Father, give this child a quiet sleep.' The child rises up and asks, a second time, for a drink of water. She again drinks, and goes off quietly to sleep. You may deny the second drink and the quiet sleep to be the result of my prayer; but you will hardly, perhaps, deny that in the providence of God it was foreseen,—I would say ordained,—that my prayer should precede the drink and the sleep; and no one accustomed to children will deny the peaceful sleep-producing influence of a peaceful and holy state of mind in those near them. You, the *Pall Mall Gazette*, seem to me to be where I was when in my youth I wrote, 'Go! in a corner whine and squeak, and let His will go by. His will is His. 'Twere also thine couldst thou but know thyself.'—A place from which I have trudged many a weary mile, and to which I would not return, no, not for all the kingdoms of the world, and the glory of them. I can but wonder at the dropping fire in such remarks as yours upon the prayers of the Roman Catholics for the temporal power, to the effect, 'Why supplement your prayers by acts?' and doubt whether, indeed, you write for earnest men or dolts."

On the latter part of this letter I need but repeat the wonder with which I regard such observations as that commented on, which, if addressed to any earnestly prayerful man, are about as markless upon him as a sentence in Hebrew on an unlearned man. If we love God our Father, and are, above all, grateful for the seemingly free powers with which He has gifted us, the most prominent desire for aid from Him is that it should be given, if possible, through those powers so seemingly our own. Who delights to bring to a friend a gift put into his hand by another so much as a gift earned by the sweat of his brow?

What earnest man that desires the temporal power of the Pope, does not desire that it should be given through his own acts, if possible, rather than fall on the Pope from heaven?

On the incident referred to in the letter, however, I must observe that the result prayed for was allowed to follow immediately on the prayer. This is not always so; not, indeed, often, as regards any outer result. An inner result, however—comparative peacefulness of mind—with me, and, I presume, with others, invariably follows prayer, if the gift of prayer be given me.

"If it be possible, let this cup pass from me," seldom removes the outer cup; but if the prayer be earnest, the nature of the cup is invariably changed by our being able to add, "Nevertheless, not as I will, but as Thou wilt," where the heroism that dares all in God's service replaces the dread that was at first inclined to regard His will as harshly unchangeable; and in how few cases would we not rather drink the cup in the spirit given, than have it removed out of regard to our dread? How much more surely, therefore, in the invariable inner answer, does God feed our truest nature than if the outer answer were the certain one. And now I feel this remark in the air about me, "How the fool talks, as if he thought we spoke and acted just as I think we speak and act, while he asserts that we really do nothing, but God all."

I do so talk, and so assert, and say that I talk and assert rightly, because—to repeat my remarks — I claim for the assertion an intellectual acknowledgment only, while I say that God, for all ordinary purposes, appoints that we should do, feel, and talk as if we did all things ourselves.

Is there, then, little attraction in prayer, if it be as I describe, and little efficacy to be expected from it, if the words be not, indeed, a voluntary address from one independent being to another?

It is useless presuming we live in a fancy world! The force of our Saviour's words, teaching that an Infinite Father, boundless in knowledge, love, and power, will be sure to be more liberal in His gifts than an earthly father, is irresistible. Our Saviour bids us, therefore, never despair, but pray always; and yet, how seldom do any of us procure by prayer the outer things we desire in the way we desire them, or with any approach to the seeming liberality with which an earthly father would respond. Some inner gift, therefore, that can be but slowly given, must obviously precede the giving of these outer gifts, or we should have but to ask, and receive. Our experience tells us what this inner gift is. Peace of mind, trust in God, and complete readiness to take whatever follows our prayer, whether in destruction or confirmation of our hopes.

Mr. Müller, with his orphanage dependent on gifts procured by prayer, does not advise others to follow his example,—clearly because he knows so few can bring the abandonment to God, trust, and faith, required. And what does abandonment to God, and trust, and faith, mean, but that we put ourselves, body and soul, into God's hands—leave him to act for us as He will? And before we can have such trust and faith, what must we believe? That, in fact, He is all in all, as I proclaim Him—that, in fact, he does govern the angry man and the good man, the devil and the angel, hell and heaven; and that therefore, in truth, the angry looks and good looks, the heavens and the earth, the air, and all we breathe, are direct from God, and full of His Spirit. We cannot have abandonment to God, trust, and faith, as I see it, without the doctrine I advocate; and if so, prayer must be of the kind I describe: and we can but bless God that, making us feel as if we were what we are not, He has given us prayer also, so needful a result of that feeling.

Am I thus making God a deceiver? The sun appears to us to revolve round the earth; the root and stem to throw off the leaves of trees, not the root and stem to be produced out of the leaves. The rain seems to us to fall from the clouds, not to condense in drops out of the whole body of the air. To a childish philosopher, the condensation on the window-panes appears to have come through the glass. To a physician, the symptoms of consumption appear those of bronchitis, and the patient dies. Does God deceive in these cases? Does He not rather, knowing that we shall be so mistaken, leave it to time and philosophy to correct our errors?

But it may be said, "No ill effects follow while we live under the above delusions, except in the last case mentioned, where the acknowledged different opinions of men warn us to distrust our conclusions." And what ill effect has followed from the faith of men that they had free-will, when they had not? The ill effect, if there be any, will rather be in the discovery of the contrary; and it is the purpose of all I write, to show this discovery as a good rather than an ill. The clear, distinct, undeniable impression that we have free-will, is no greater than our clear impression as to a thousand natural phenomena about which we are mistaken. How, then, does God deceive in the one more than in the other? You are not satisfied? "No! To produce the nature you describe—your free-will—an organized system of deception must exist on all sides of us; a system that would fail in its purpose if it did not deceive. Admitting that God foreknew we should suppose the sun to revolve round the earth, and yet did so make us and the sun, you cannot say it is vital to our being that we should be so deceived; but of free-will you do say this—you say that faith in the deception is the heart of all social existence—is our glory. Is this possible? Can God be such a one as to deceive us, and make our faith in the deceit essential to our being?"

If God be the real owner of all things, and we but the apparent owners, "deceit" of the kind you refer to is inherent in all human ownership.

For the free nature of which I speak substitute flocks and herds, lands and houses, food and drink; these we are ready to maintain ours at the sword's point, and yet the uncertainty of their possession marks them ours only in appearance—somewhat more mine than yours, but mine in no sense wholly,—death, fire, robbery, a thousand events we call accidental, may at any moment deprive me of my seeming possession. The custom is to call all these things God's, as indeed they are. How comes all this? Surely the "deceit" is as great in making our relationship toward them such that, while they seem our own, we have yet to acknowledge the uncertainty of their possession makes them God's. I would not, however, be understood to assert that faith in free-will, or any other possession, is produced in us by appearances, but that such faith is God's direct gift to us—a gift which more than any other entitles us to be called God's children—and that the outer world is created as it were through us, and assumes the form which it must assume to be accordant with this gift. With the first scream of the infant its sense of ownership comes into the world. It cannot be otherwise, then, than inborn.

And now I must fall back on conjugial love. When this love is perfect, the woman gives herself to the man so completely that he feels her inspirations in himself as his own. We call this the perfection of love; we do not call it deceit.

While we intellectually ascribe to the wife the heaven-born female nature with which we are possessed, there would be no love did we not appropriate, adopt, feel the nature as our own. That God intends us to feel His nature, as given to us in the same way, we have abundant proof in many passages of His Word. I need not quote more than one. Our Lord prays for His disciples, "That they all may be one, as thou, Father, art in me, and I in thee, that they also may be one in us." *

Assume, then, that God does thus give us His nature,—that He gives us our momentary thoughts, words, and deeds, making them feel in us as our own—and that He makes the world without assume the form which it must assume to be accordant with the inner state we thus receive through His utter abandonment of Himself to us in love,—is this deceit? If the appropriation of God's nature were produced in us by the operation upon us of the creation outside, it would be produced by deceit; as would the wife's influence with the husband, if produced by her deeds, instead of sealed and confirmed by them — deeds that spring from her absorption in his interests. If her loving life were deliberately planned to

---

* This prayer I understand to be simply one for illumination. We are always really one with God. The prayer, therefore, is answered when we are made to perceive the unity.

create in the husband the false feeling that he possessed her nature, she would, in the same way, be trying to deceive him. In true conjugial love, however, we all know that this is not so, but that the felt union produces the deeds. And if, talking, as we must, from appearances, we do not intellectually correct our words, but regard God as planning the outside world in order to re-act on man and produce in him false impressions, we also ascribe deceit to God; but if we regard Him as giving Himself to man in the abandonment of love, and creating the outer world through the combined divine and human nature, there is simply concordance—not deceit.

In the light of this apprehension I read the first chapter of John, where, speaking of the Word that "was made flesh," it is written, "In the beginning was the Word, and the Word was with God, and the Word was God. The same was in the beginning with God. All things were made by Him; and without Him was not anything made that was made. In Him was life; and the life was the light of men. And the light shineth in darkness;

and the darkness comprehended it not." In these words I see the statement that the outer world was created through the combined being, God and man, just as home is created through the combined man and wife; and the creation being from within outwards, I can see no more deceit in the one creation than in the other.

Without under-estimating, however, the importance of regarding the world outside as formed from the world within, God's dealing with us, after all, comes to this,—He so gives Himself to us that He makes things that are His appear ours. Looking boldly at this statement, we must admit that, if so to deal with us be deceitful, it certainly is deceit of a kind of which we can neither receive nor give too much. Let us, then, thank God that while He breathes the prayer that speeds upwards, He has given us souls that can love and appropriate the words, and feel that we are rightly called children, and He our Father. Let us learn to know Him by that name which sums up all explanation in one word—" Love."*

* Hence the central nature of God's marriage with the Church, and my dedication of this book.

On the Word of God.

IF God be, in fact, the only one present—the speaker and doer of all we call good and of all we call evil—how can any book be especially called the Word of God?

The mixture here of good and evil deprives all ordinary speech and writing, every ordinary thought, deed, sight, and breath, of being what we characterize as divine; for by divine we mean that which breathes of heaven alone.

Since God made hell as well as heaven, and since the earth invites gusts from hell as well as the breeze of heaven, anything born of earth, earthy in its nature, blows, like the satyr's guest, a double breath. From the side of heaven the whole structure of the earth tends heavenwards; from the side of hell, hellwards. Now, if the daily events of the world can be related from the side of heaven, those aspects of things will alone be regarded, those tendencies alone dwelt on, that influence alone outbreathed from the history which points heavenwards. If such a book were written, we should discover it by its influence upon us being heavenwards; and such a book the Bible is to me,—ever correcting weak sentimentalism, ever encouraging me in distress, and breathing in me a new faith and trust in God my Father, omnipotent, omniscient, omnipresent.

Through the air made dim and vaporous by the confused mixture of good and evil—of the man in whom is being inbreathed preponderating love of God and the neighbour, with the man in whom the love of self and the world is being made to daily gain the mastery—this "revelation," this "Word of God," shines before us as a sun, and draws its shelter round us as a shield; its heat breathes warm life upon our spirits; its strength—which calls us not away from the world, but from the evil—gives us a living defence; and the influence of its story is so full of a growth keeping pace with our wants, that we become no more anxious about the result of scientific inquiry than fearful that the research which discovers spots upon the material sun will rob it of its heat and life-giving power. We come, indeed, to hail the inquirer, and revel in his discoveries, because they must correct exuberant fancies, trim God's Word of the dimming influence of man's additions: for men are prone to seek—even arrogantly to require—that God's works shall *seem to them* perfect,—forgetful that, as we have seen, their very perfection may need the presence of what seems imperfect.

Arithmetical puzzles and inaccuracies in God's works may thus crop up before one generation, spots on the sun's disc, placed there to lead men to a joyful life, giving indifference to the letter that kills, and force them, willing or unwilling, to bask only in the heat of the Spirit that gives life.

If all the world's a stage, and men and women merely players, history is but an account of the drama acted; and the Old Testament and the New contain this drama as enacted in the part of Jewish history related. They are books written for the edification of the heavenly man, and regard all things with his eyes. We thus have hell described as a place "where their worm dieth not, and the fire is not quenched;" a "furnace of fire; there shall be wailing and gnashing of teeth;" a place of "everlasting fire, prepared for the devil and his angels;" a place of "everlasting punishment,"—all accounts of hell as it appears to the heavenly man. Even of Judas Iscariot our Lord says, "It had been good for that man if he had not been born;" not that he—a mere puppet in God's hands, doing a deed, villanous, it is true, but one by which all men are blessed—will not go to his happiness, like the rest of his race; but that to the heavenly man his offence is such, that the worst of all imaginable things—annihilation—were preferable.

I call Jewish history an account of a drama, containing a set of appearances which are to their deeper meaning, surface appearances. I must give it this name, because God really moves, while man seems to move, the actors.

I feel myself specially entitled to call this history, with its central event of the crucifixion, a drama: for I find the one crucified, Himself telling His disciples, that whatever be done to Him, it is not men that do it, but Himself only, as the human embodiment of God.

"Therefore doth my Father love me, because I lay down my life that I might take it again; no man taketh it from me, but I lay it down of myself." He thus warns His disciples, "Be not deceived by appearances; look beneath the surface of things; never mind that men seem to do all you will see done, of themselves: they are but puppets in my hands and my Father's, and play the parts we appoint. Their acting, it is true, calls forth real blood, genuine tears, heartfelt joy. We will it so; and, behold, I, even I, do not shrink from all We have appointed. I, the Director, have become a seeming actor among you for a time, and see, according to our laws, I suffer and die even as you suffer and die, and joy and live even as you joy and live." And in His own words, "Let not your heart be troubled: ye believe in God, believe also in me."

In His body's youth, too—it is well we should not forget—our Lord suffered temptation through being Himself deceived by the seeming reality and independence of the world about Him, even as we also are deceived and tempted.

And now, should it be said, If your theory of the world be true, and in conformity with Scripture, why do we not find Scripture phrases more carefully worded, consorting more fully with it?

The answer reveals one of the most subtle features of divinity in the Bible. All that I and ordinary men write is tainted with our mortality, by being either over or understated, or somewhat misstated, so that it serves the race for a time, and then is thrown aside as a worn-out coat, to be replaced by a newer garment of more recent fashion—an equally perishable new theory grown out of the old, and suited to increased intelligence. These perishable truths are like the scientific nomenclature and conclusions of the natural philosopher,—so soon affected by the growth of knowledge that new nomenclatures arise almost before the old are well used, and new encyclopædias become necessary almost before the old ones are completed. The Bible, on the other hand, is like the productions of Nature herself, as unchangeable, containing a use for the hand of the workman, an affection for the soul of the poet, and the substance of all religious philosophy. If, then, the Bible receives any fresh illumination from my theory, I expect no more. I do not expect to find its statements one-sided, as I am sure mine are, and to find them, in order not to touch the heels of the true theory of appearances, introducing confusion in a thousand different ways.

For myself, indeed, under the double influence of the Bible and modern philosophy, I find from the views set forth herein, not simply assistance, but absolutely no escape. So complete and searching is God's government, as expounded in the Bible, that men must, to my apprehension, be mere puppets in God's hands, if, on the theory that we are puppets, a satisfactory account can be given of ourselves and the world.

On Law.

THAT we may seem to be independent actors in the world, God's doings must be so fashioned that our intellects can grasp, arrange, and anticipate them—that we can seemingly compare notes together, and assist each other in foretelling events. The object, then, of law is not that we may take advantage of the laws of nature, but that God may be able to make us appear to ourselves so to do—that we may seem to write books, calculate, and tabulate.

Did not God move according to such rules as we can follow and understand, the instinct we obeyed would be indeed as blind as that of the animal. We could never be made to seem to revel in the realm of invention as we now do; we could never seem to grow in intelligence and knowledge—never seem to understand better our God and Father; and giving us no knowledge of Himself, He could not make us feel as if we held communion with Him. It is by keeping His movements according to rule that He enables either angel or devil to exist. As, therefore, the Sabbath is made for the use of man, so also is law—not man made in order that he may be subject to law.

Demonstration of the prevalence of law in science already abounds. The same prevalence of law is found in human character. While each of us receives momentary inspiration from God, that inspiration is ever given in a series seeming to evolve a character—a character becoming daily, with the consent of its reasoning faculties, and therefore apparently by its own choice, more and more consistent with the experiences stored up in the memory, the inconsistencies which are being cleared away, resulting from the double constitution of the world, so often referred to—or, as we term it, from the existence of evil; and these inconsistencies being necessary—at all events in the early stage of our being—to give the world without that form it would take, had we the free-will we have but in seeming,—to give us, in fact, a seeming choice. We are—to repeat my theme—shown what an angel and what a devil is, and then led into angelhood or devilhood with the delight and rapturous applause of our whole being at our escape from the painful knowledge of our opposite.

Just again, as each individual's thoughts and acts are arranged so as to build up a character which is distinctive, so the thoughts and acts of the family evolve also a distinctive family character, and the thoughts and acts of the nation a national character. All the acts in which a family unite are the results of the family character. In the infancy of the children this character is little more than the united character of father and mother: as the children exert more influence, their peculiarities affect the family character and its influence; and were an artist to attempt to symbolize in one figure that family, he would doubtless draw a human figure, the main lines of which resulted from

H

the combined character of father and mother; and if he drew his picture truly, modifying the austerity in the father's brow by the affection of the wife, by the life and hopefulness of the children,—or by the soberness and tender care introduced if any permanent invalid were in the family,—a judge of character would be able to foretell the family action on any question. Would any subscription be furnished by that house for such a purpose? Would Jane Smith be a suitable servant for that family? Would such and such trades-people be the ones to serve them? How would they act in such a law-suit?

It is similar with the national character; and such an artist as described, could he draw a picture of the nation, would draw that human being from whom, for the moment, could be deduced the action of the nation; or he would draw the real king of that nation, a king whose will has been attempted to be ascertained by registering votes, and in a thousand ways; a king whose acts are the result of the meditation and activity of the national thinking faculties; a king whose desires and intentions are sometimes more clearly seen, by some one man who, feeling sure of his knowledge, seizes upon power, than arrived at by the voting urn.

Perhaps the ideal king of a meditative internal nature requires generations to pass in talk and reflection, and then becomes ripe to spread his power and influence beneath the guidance of a Frederick the Great or a Bismarck.

Perhaps, weary of revolution and an unreal desire for universal brotherhood, the king, ever changeable in his mood, rules the nation by the wise despotism of a Louis Napoleon. No ruler, however, can exist as ruler longer than he is able to read the orders of the ideal king.

Now this ideal king, so long as the world is formed of heaven-bound and hell-bound, can never be God Himself as we know Him in His human form of Christ; for the king of hell is Satan, and Satan's future subjects will ever long for a satanic ruler,—one who can give them pomp and show, one who can flatter their vanity, one who can bribe them, put them into comfortable sinecures, one who will reward the spy, one who will pay for the doings of hell in the coin of hell.

There will ever, therefore—so long as the world is constituted as it is—be a Cæsar to receive the things that are Cæsar's. Not that a ruler is needfully of infernal nature, but he must be of a nature very evenly balanced; and having to select out of the two types, the choice will certainly often fall on the infernal character; and I need not appeal to any great knowledge of history to show that, in fact, the choice does generally so fall.

A ruler of the good type, should the choice fall on him, must certainly have infernal helpmates, who can supplement his wants towards their fellows. While assured, therefore, that we shall never find the decidedly good man in high places, we must be content to see the evil man there, and always anticipate having to keep him and his doings in order, through fear of exposure and loss of place, when speaking of a ruler,—"the right man in the right place" being, in fact, the man whose nature is such that he must give this trouble.

Thus does law run through all human nature and all society, and thus, law ruling, while acting every moment at the direct inspiration of God, while, in fact, speaking and doing His words and deeds only, we can understand His proceedings, and be made to feel all the changes He is producing—all the growth He is creating—as changes and growth created and produced by ourselves.

CONCLUSION.

EXAMPLES.

SOME friends of mine have for years employed me on many matters of business. A large business engagement of theirs, I believe I could do well, seems likely to be put in my hands. I am partly employed upon it, when, in an outspoken, careless fashion, I relate some occurrences which took place between me and a personage important to conciliate in their interest. Little remark is made for the time; but it becomes obvious that the matter has been talked over among them, and they have determined—erroneously, in my opinion—that, for the present, the more eminent and influential personage, also partly in their employ, shall take the whole business in hand.

Months roll on, and beyond occasional slight reference to the matter, no further communications take place between us. Business becomes dull. I know something must be doing by them which I feel sure I could do better than he who I believe is doing it, and who is himself oppressed with work; and I trace the whole to my hasty, outspoken account of an interview.

And now, how does all anxiety and annoyance vanish when I correct deceitful appearances by my intellectual theory, and acknowledge that God has spoken through me and through them in the whole transaction. That He it is uttered the outspoken remarks, that He allowed the impression—I think mistaken—to take root in their minds, and that He Himself has been the only agent in all the subsequent events, and appointed it all for our good. My annoyance is changed into a feeling of humility and trust—into the perception that the only thing to desire is a heavenly state of mind—that this is the treasure "hid in a field, the which when a man hath found, he hideth, and for joy thereof goeth and selleth all that he hath, and buyeth that field."

A man whom I, as the agent of his landlord, urge to perform the works he is bound to perform by his lease, says the demand is arbitrary, and asks for an explanation of a certain transaction which took place three or four years ago, and which he says throws the burden of the work on his landlord. I write him a letter in reply, setting forth the whole transaction referred to, as far as my papers throw light upon it, and suppose the objection at an end. The man calls on me, showers around him complaints on the hardness of the engagements by which he was bound to do this work—engagements which he yet voluntarily incurred—storms at the rapacity of his landlord, accuses me of negligence, threatens suits at law, details the case he will make out—for which my letter of explanations has, I find, through its good-natured explicitness, become the chief authority—and when he is gone, and I think over the interview, I believe he has been attempting to get further confessions for use against my landlord and me.

I relate, I daresay, an every-day business occurrence, and one that most men would laugh at; but it leaves on me a very painful impression, in which I blame my own good-nature and open-heartedness; but when I reflect that the words I wrote were not mine, but our Father's—that the man who has left me, in the use he would make of them, is but obeying the nature our Father has put in him, and in all he has done and will do he is alike acting direct from our Father—all my anxiety vanishes. I feel that I am where I am intended to be, have heard what I was intended to hear, and shall be called on to do that, and that only, which God alike appoints and directs.

I have a piece of duty to perform, which is likely to lead to hot contention with an unscrupulous and violent opponent. The duty must be performed, or I fail in my trust. The gloom of the possible coming contention clouds the passing days. I bid myself be bold, point out that there is no escape—and yet I find little comfort. The gloom will not be driven away; the clouds will not be dispelled. The air about me seems to resound with lamentations that I was born ———; but when I think that the pure God who hates iniquity is as much on the other side as on mine,—is as regardful of the other's good as of mine—as He governs my movements, so also governs the in-goings and out-comings of the violent man—appoints or forbids our meeting as is absolutely best for the imperishable in both—that every word spoken and every deed done will really be the word and deed of the pure God,—I feel how vain is my fear. Through all the savage looks and deeds purity reigns triumphant, and a final victory over that which each feels as evil for the angel or for the devil.

To sum up all examples in one,—If dearest friends die, and we trace their death to our errors; if ruin overtakes us, and we trace it to our blunders; if friends fall away and solitude darkens about us,—whatever evil happens, no cure for regret is so perfect as the faith that these things were to be; and if they have come through our blunders, that we should blunder has been as inevitable, as distinctly directed and intended by our Father, as that the sun should rise.

God omnipotent, omniscient, omnipresent, He gives anxiety and care, self-reproach and doubt; if we would have the rewards of their coming, we must be brave to bear them, and the time of our deliverance is near, when we see their unfittingness to that we would and believe we shall become when—speaking in the language of those appearances in which He makes His doings pass before us—we recognize them as vaporous uprisings from the pit beneath.

Crash after crash come the trials of the world. Repose, if we look for it, we shall not find, but the branch which shows itself above the stormy flood, and gives a foothold, is faith in God omnipotent, omniscient, omnipresent.

Summary.

THIS, then, is the world I see—all gaiety and wealth, all filth * and all oppression,—every loveable and every loathsome thing alike resulting from God's presence;—the mighty drama so acted that men may see before them a mass of contention, suffering, and struggle,—a mass of evil ripe for their sickle and the fire—evil that in God's hands works good results before it is destroyed, no other way attainable—that makes men heroes, and gives them in its destruction the feeling that

* How well Lord Palmerston said, "Dirt is but matter in the wrong place." It appears before us as dirt, that, seeing it put in the right place, we may, without despising anything God has made, know when matter became dirt.

they have laboured for and produced great results, every one of which is God's doing; not a single one theirs.

I see the work of God handed over to men as if their own,—His hand everywhere; nothing without Him.

I see Him not glorying in the good and shrinking not back from the evil, but breathing life into all, and calmly ever moving onwards to foreordained results.

I see each man taking day by day the special form God intends him each day to bear: a creature of many cares, who need have none; a creature of many fears, to whom all fear is folly, racked with anxiety about bubbles.

I see the breath of God breathing over him every care, fear, anxiety, and trouble, and himself enjoying, as the result, the glorious delusion that he makes and unmakes, does and undoes, invents, contrives, and lives in a state of independence God cannot delegate.

EPILOGUE.

"EVERY scribe which is instructed unto the kingdom of heaven is like unto a man that is an householder, which bringeth forth out of his treasure things new and old."

THUS God the Bridegroom is, the Church
    the Bride—
A mystic Bride, in heavenly outline mapped,
Whose gentle form majestic folds about
The wise and simple, every mortal man,
Of every people, nation, tongue, and clime,
With forehead stamped by seal of holy God.
To breathe the tale of love to a whole race
Is the affection of each single one,
To woo with tender word and sweet embrace.
The cheerful voice of children in the gale,
Which e'en on foreign soil, where Turk is met
With sword and pistol dangling at his belt,

Seem still the well-known music of our home,—
Tell of responsive echo to God's voice
In their most dear familiar melody;
Tell of that grand Bridegroom whose whispers fall
So gently that the spiritual ear
Of the dear bridal race alone they reach.*
They reach, and are not recognized, yet train,
Of the sealed race, each trembling ignorant child
To lisp on loving lips God's glorious name;
And day by day earth's nature from the child,—
Which starts and shrinks from the sharp piercing pain
His nature bids it bear, and mopes and whines
And shivers at the God,—they purge away,
Till, grasping now God's hand, with holy love—
As for the Lamb that dared and died—'tis filled.
The whisper heard is God's, who breathes all life

* The statements herein cannot be made of the evil race, who, however freely they may seem to choose their daily course, are always governed by considerations of expediency and self-interest—can never be abandoned in that wifely trust in God which through love and faith casteth out fear.

In Christian, Turk, Hindoo, and Chinaman;
In lion, tiger, crocodile, and lamb;
In little bird that warbles on the spray—
The bridal life still central everywhere.
The sound of marriage-bells along the vale
Proclaim of man with maid this life begun,—
A life he'd make for her one summer's day.
His the Grand Bridegroom's love in mortal
    measure,—
Love of which He who sends the winter's storm,
Pouring direct from the great central ocean,
With arm outstretched flings forth the living
    streams
In dread and glory decked,—delight and pain,
Joy, hunger, death, till every sighing thought
In men—from puny children heroes made—
He wins alone. Men with Him filled always
Know not His whisper till they love Him thus.
Then God within in every thought they find,
No other speech nor voice than His they hear,
No other eye they see, no other form,
No other breath they feel, nor touch, nor sigh.
Ah! weep ye, weep at wooing of your Lord,
Ye yet in heaven will wake in loving, daring
    Him—

In heaven, a state of soul that loveth to the
    death.
Ah ! then a crown of glory you are made—
In God's right hand a royal diadem ;
No more forsaken, no more desolate ;
Then, as from One who worketh perfect things,
Bright show you gain to clothe dark substance
    o'er.
So unto Husband God you wife become—
To Husband that with holy wife is one ;
One with your God in hope, in heart, in home,
Whose all things are, and all that is—your own.